W9-AAA-728

B219631029

THE CH   OK

ELMWOOD PARK PUBLIC LIBRARY
4 CONTI PARKWAY
ELMWOOD PARK, IL 60707
(708) 453-7645/8236

1. A fine is charged for each day a book is kept beyond the due date. The Library Board may take legal action if books are not returned within three months.
2. Books damaged beyond reasonable wear shall be paid for.
3. Each borrower is responsible for all books charged on this card and for all fines accruing on the same.

⅞ 618.928521
⁄01 MIL
Mil c.'

THE CHILDHOOD DEPRESSION SOURCEBOOK

by
Jeffrey A. Miller, Ph.D.

LOWELL HOUSE

LOS ANGELES

NTC/Contemporary Publishing Group

MGM

ELMWOOD PARK PUBLIC LIBRARY
4 CONTI PARKWAY
ELMWOOD PARK, IL. 60635
453-7645/8235

Library of Congress Cataloging-in-Publication Data

Miller, Jeffrey A., 1965–
   The childhood depression sourcebook / by Jeffrey A. Miller.
         p.   cm.
   Includes index.
   ISBN 0-7373-0001-9
   1. Depression in children—Popular works. 2. Depression in
adolescence—Popular works.   I. Title.
   RJ506.D4M55   1998
   618.92'8527—dc21   98-45345
                                                    CIP

Published by Lowell House, a division of NTC/Contemporary
Publishing Group, Inc., 4255 West Touhy Avenue, Lincolnwood,
Illinois 60646-1975 U.S.A.

Copyright © 1998 by NTC/Contemporary Publishing Group.
All rights reserved. No part of this work may be reproduced, stored in
a retrieval system, or transmitted in any form or by any means electronic,
mechanical, photocopying, recording, or otherwise without prior permission
of NTC/Contemporary Publishing Group, Inc.

Design by S. Pomeroy.

Printed and bound in the United States of America

International Standard Book Number: 0-7373-0001-9

10 9 8 7 6 5 4 3 2 1

To my colleague and friend, Dr. Michael Tansy

CONTENTS

PREFACE

Depression is a serious problem among our youth. Although children with depression were not treated for many years, they are finally being recognized and helped. The most current research on depression is resulting in better pharmacological and psychological treatments for depression. It is encouraging, too, that the developing information about its causes is providing real answers about how to prevent depression in children. A barrier to the dissemination of this information is the general lack of knowledge about how to identify children that are depressed and the ways parents, school personnel, and others important in children's lives can significantly reduce their suffering. The purpose of this book is to provide information about depression in a relatively nontechnical manner and raise awareness about depression in children.

In the first chapter I provide a selective overview of the history of childhood depression, a general description of the symptoms of depression in children, and an organizing theory on which to build throughout the rest of the book. Chapter 2 covers the explicit definitions of childhood depression and its associated symptoms, and a detailed description of how psychologists and psychiatrists make the diagnosis of depression. It is hoped that this will demystify the process of psychological assessment and encourage parents to have their children evaluated if depression is suspected. In chapter 3 the different depression theories are described with an emphasis on applying them to real life.

Chapter 4 covers the various other emotional problems that tend to occur with depression. Children are prone to anxiety, disruptive behavior, and substance abuse in conjunction with depression, and it is important to understand the features of these different problems. The broad spectrum of depression treatment is covered in chapter 5. It is my intent in that chapter to describe the most accepted and effective professional treatments for depression without idealizing trendy but unproven therapies.

Chapters 6, 7, and 8 are concerned with what you as a family member or significant person in a depressed child's life can do to help. What to do when a depressed child acts in extreme and sometimes frightening ways is described in chapter 6. What schools can offer a depressed child and how to access these services is discussed in chapter 7. Chapter 8 provides explicit information about how to parent a child with depression and how to prevent childhood depression when possible.

It is my sincere hope that we all gain a better understanding of childhood depression to facilitate its early identification and treatment. I am indebted to Lowell House for the opportunity to help make this happen. I also would like to thank the many mentors and teachers who have helped me better understand childhood depression. Finally, I would like to acknowledge the many children and adolescents I have worked with who have shared their inner experiences and helped me develop empathy for their challenges. I invite readers to share their thoughts on this book and on childhood depression with me via e-mail at millerjeff@duq.edu.

JEFFREY A. MILLER
Duquesne University
Pittsburgh, Pennsylvania

I am in that temper that if I were under water
I would scarcely kick to come to the top.
—John Keats on depression, May 1818

CHAPTER 1

OVERVIEW OF CHILDHOOD DEPRESSION

Depression can have a devastating impact on children's lives. It affects how they feel and behave at home, at school, with their friends, and for adolescents, at work. Until relatively recently, depression in children was not widely accepted as a real disorder. As a result, the scientific research necessary to understand how children experience depression, why they get depressed, and how to help them has emerged only in the last twenty years. Thankfully, since the beginning of the era of critical evaluation of childhood depression, dramatic strides toward understanding this disorder have been made and substantial hope can be offered to children with depression and to their families.

The diagnosis of depression can be confusing because there are several different kinds of depression. The two main categories of depression are unipolar and bipolar. *Unipolar* means the person only feels "down" and experiences the classic symptoms of depression, including feeling worthless, poor appetite, sleep disturbance, lack of motivation, and suicidal thoughts. *Bipolar* means the individual experiences down periods as well as manic episodes characterized by elevated mood, inflated self-esteem, talkativeness, and rapidly changing thoughts. *Depression* is a cyclical disorder with periods of relief or well-being interspersed among periods of either depression only or depression and mania. Sometimes there is only one episode of depression, but, in most cases, particularly with children, more than one episode occurs.

Children and adolescents with depression experience four main classes of disturbances: problems with thoughts, emotions, behavior, and physiological processes. Problems with thinking include difficulty concentrating, indecisiveness, thoughts of death, feelings of worthlessness, and excessive guilt. Problems with emotions include having a depressed mood, irritability, reduced interest or pleasure in activities, and a lack of emotional expression or variability. Problems with behavior include agitation or lethargy. Finally, physiological symptoms include sleeping too much or too little, decreased or increased appetite, fatigue, and lack of energy. These are the features or symptoms that a psychologist or psychiatrist identifies to make the diagnosis of depression.

How an individual child truly experiences or manifests depression and how the depression impacts her life can be highly variable. In addition, children may have no idea that they are depressed. Since they are experiencing the world for the first time and have only limited comparative information, they may actually think that depression is absolutely normal. This has to do with the egocentric nature of children's thoughts. For example, if they were raised in the city it is reasonable for them to think that all children live in the city or that the whole world looks like the city. In the same way, children with depression may believe all children feel depressed. Unfortunately, parents with limited experience may commit the same error and think that the depressive symptoms their child displays are normal and that all children experience them. This, however, is not the case.

It is important to understand the differences between the researcher's, the therapist's, and the child's perspective on depression in order to best support your child through the trials of this common, but often devastating, illness. In this chapter I will provide an integrated overview of childhood depression and develop a framework from which you can assimilate the information in the rest of the book or that you may be exposed to from a variety of other sources in the future.

YES, CHILDREN DO GET DEPRESSED

Recent studies indicate that as many as 2.5 percent of children and 8.5 percent of adolescents experience depression. Given these relatively high prevalence rates, it may be surprising to note that it was not widely accepted that children experienced depression until the 1970s. In 1970, Warren Weinberg and his colleagues developed the first diagnostic criteria for depression in which the developmental differences between children and adults were considered. Widespread research on childhood depression did not begin until the late 1970s, following Weinberg's better specification of the diagnosis and the dissipating of historical misconceptions about childhood depression, such as "masked depression."

The modern diagnosis and treatment of adult mental illness began in the late 1800s with the birth of the field of psychology. Why did it take so long to understand that children could also suffer from depression, the "common cold" of mental illness? The highly influential work of Sigmund Freud accounts for much of the reason children were not diagnosed with depression for about fifty years. In 1917, Freud believed that depression included, among other things, the "lowering of the self-regarding feelings" and "delusional expectation of punishment." He theorized that children did not have the capacity for self-regard (superego functioning) or the ability to envision the future sufficiently to have feelings of hopelessness. Thus, children could not become depressed.

During adolescence it was believed that youth did have the necessary personality development to experience depression. Despite this, prior to the 1970s, depressive symptoms in adolescents were considered a normal part of adolescent development by some theorists. For example, D.W. Winnicott identified the "doldrum" phase in adolescence as being necessary for healthy emotional development. We know now that depression is not a normal part of development for adolescents or anyone.

Finally, in the 1960s, researchers began to accept the existence of depression in children. However, these researchers segregated themselves into two groups with divergent theories. One camp felt depression in children was much like that in adults. That is, children experienced depressed mood, negative self-concept, self-depreciation, sleeping and eating changes, and withdrawal. The other group believed that children experienced depression but that it was "masked" behind symptoms not typically seen in adult depression. In young children, depression was thought to be masked by symptoms of tantrums, school phobia, and defiance. In older children, depression was marked by restlessness, boredom, delinquency, aggression, and anxiety. Theorists supporting masked depression thought that traditional symptoms of depression would not be exhibited until the late teens. The masked depression group ultimately did not convince most researchers, and this notion has since fallen by the wayside. Although children with depression may exhibit some symptoms historically described as masked depression, this catchall diagnosis did not serve to differentiate childhood depression from other forms of childhood emotional problems. Such catchall terms do not help to forward the research necessary to determine how to treat a disorder.

Since the 1970s, when childhood depression was first described with strict diagnostic criteria, there has been general consensus that children exhibit depressive symptoms similar to those of adults, with some of the features identified as masked depression. Specifically, irritability can replace depressed mood in making the diagnosis for children. The most current research in the area of comparative diagnosis of depression between children and adults has been conducted by Dr. Maria Kovacs with the Western Psychiatric Institute and Clinic in Pittsburgh. Her research will be covered in a subsequent section, but, in summary, she found that the clinical presentation of depression in children is very similar to that of adults.

This account of the history of childhood depression may suggest that no one was attuned to depressive symptoms in children before the 1960s. This, however, is not true; several professionals noticed depressive symptoms in children while working in other areas, such as physical illness and attachment in children. This work is very helpful for understanding some of the more subtle aspects of depression discussed later in this book.

In the late 1950s, a pediatrician, Dr. Leon Cytryn, noticed that children hospitalized for surgery sometimes showed sadness and withdrawal. He conducted several studies and discovered that almost 50 percent of children with chronic medical problems experienced symptoms of depression including sadness, withdrawal, helplessness, hopelessness, and social isolation. These children also experienced symptoms of anxiety including separation anxiety, avoidance, irritability, sleep disturbances, and phobias. Dr. Cytryn's early work is important in several respects. First, he predicted the presence of the same depression disorder experienced by adults in children. Second, he observed that children experience depression caused by one's situation, called reactive depression; that is, when people are exposed to very stressful events or conditions, they may become depressed. Finally, he noticed the close relationship between symptoms of depression and symptoms of anxiety in children. This final notion (mixed anxiety and depression) represents one of the most important areas to be addressed by depression researchers for the next decade.

In 1946, René Spitz described a phenomenon known as "anaclitic depression." Infants separated from their mothers at the age of six months to one year showed a sad face, withdrawal, failure to interact, and refusal to eat. John Bowlby also found that children between the ages of six months and three years exhibited withdrawal, a sad face, whimpering, and refusal to eat when separated from their mothers. Infant and toddler depressive responses showed that traumatic incidents experienced even in this early stage of cognitive development can result in depressivelike episodes. Recent research on genetic and environmental causes of depression suggests that these emotional stressors may initiate a biologically predisposed cycle of depression. This work will be discussed later and represents another important area of childhood depression research for the coming decade.

At this time there is no question that children can and do get depressed. Now that we know childhood depression exists, one needs to know how prevalent it is. Of children between the ages of seven and twelve years, referred for mental health services, approximately 10 to 20 percent experience depression. In random samples of children not referred for mental health services, depression was found in up to 2.5 percent of children and up to 8.5 percent of adolescents. This indicates that the prevalence of depression varies as a function of age and implies the existence of some developmental correlates of depression, such as puberty and cognitive development.

The prevalence of depression also varies by gender. Depressive symptoms were twice as common in boys among prepubertal children between the ages of seven and twelve years. Depressive symptoms were twice as common, however, in girls among postpubertal children older than twelve years. This consistent finding in depression research suggests that genetic, biological, social, and cultural factors are related to depression.

By late adolescence, youth get depressed with similar frequency and gender patterns as adults. The fact that the symptoms of depression are similar in children and adults and that its prevalence is similar among adolescents and adults does not mean that the manifestation of depression is the same for children and adults. The constellation of depressive symptoms, associated or comorbid disorders, rates of recovery, and patterns of relapse are actually different for children than adults.

ADULT VERSUS CHILDHOOD DEPRESSION

Aside from diagnostic similarities, there are several important differences between adult and childhood depression. Most of these differences were discovered by Dr. Kovacs. One rather obvious difference is that, when diagnosed in children, the depressive episode is typically the first, while adults frequently have experienced several depressive episodes. This has two implications. The first is good for children; that is, early identification and treatment of depression are associated with better adjustment later on. The second is not so good. Multiple episodes of depression, especially if untreated, are associated with poor outcomes. Since children experience their first depressive episodes so young, the probability that they will have more episodes is high. There is emerging developmental research that suggests there is a cumulative effect of repeated depressive episodes; these cause an individual to become depressed more easily and severely in the future. Therefore, there is great advantage to noticing the symptoms of depression early and providing immediate treatment.

Unfortunately, childhood depression is underidentified, and many children go untreated. A number of emotional and behavioral disorders in children go unnoticed until a child enters formal education. However, children with depression are often quiet, compliant, and not disorderly. Although their grades may not be good, they seldom get referred for help because they are not disruptive to the teaching environment. They usually only receive help when they act drastically such as being frequently truant, becoming angry or frustrated in class, or attempting suicide. Also, with depression, the occurrence of a depressive episode may not happen until the child is an adolescent. Regrettably, as we have seen with early theorists, the emergence of depressive symptoms is often considered a normal or at least expected part of adolescent development. As a result, the teenager is not given the necessary help.

Although seemingly contradictory, children who have had a depressive episode are less likely than adults to have another depressive episode. This is really just an artifact of the differences in developmental stages of depression among child and adult samples. Research has shown that approximately 70 percent of children identified as having a depressive episode will have a recurrence of depression. However, adults will have a recurrent episode of depression up to 90 percent of the time. This difference is accounted for by the fact that most adults have already had multiple depressive episodes (the major predictor of future episodes). Nonetheless, in research samples, a recurrence of depression was found almost 100 percent of the time if someone with childhood depression had at least one new episode of depression after age seventeen. So, if the first depressive episode occurs in childhood, it should be considered serious in terms of chances for recurrence.

As I have said, recurrence is related to poor treatment outcomes. There is a well-known associated feature of recurrence of depression that was noticed in adults by Emil Kraeplin in the late 1800s. He saw that the period of normalcy between depressive episodes became shorter with each successive episode. That is, each new depressive episode came faster than the last. Kraeplin also noticed that the first episode of depression was triggered by a fairly major stressor, but that subsequent episodes did not require as much stress to induce a depressive episode.

When depressed people experience their first depressive episode during childhood, they are at greater risk for moving from unipolar depression to bipolar depression. In adults, about 10 percent of those with major depression develop bipolar depression. In children, the conversion from unipolar to bipolar depression occurs in 20 to 30 percent of cases. In some respects, this represents a more severe and difficult-to-treat emotional disturbance. This switch typically occurs during an active depressive episode but usually does not occur until the child has experienced several previous episodes of depression. If the switch is going to occur during a depressive episode, it typically takes place early in the course of that depressive phase. The typical time frame is four months from the onset of the depressive episode. This switch from unipolar to bipolar occurs approximately four months into a depressive episode for both adults and children.

Children tend to recover from their depressive episodes more quickly than adults. The typical recovery time from the onset of a depressive episode is between seven to nine months for children and about twelve months for adults. This seemingly positive feature of childhood depression is offset by the fact that early onset is indicative of a poorer clinical course in terms of recurrence and switching to bipolar disorder.

STRESS AND DEPRESSION

When something stressful happens in a child's life, he may suffer a temporary disruption in daily functioning. Incidents such as parental divorce, illness in the family, moving, the birth of a sibling, or the death of a family member can lead to symptoms similar to depression. If the stressor is removed or stabilizes, however, and the depressive symptoms subside within six months, the term *adjustment disorder* rather than depression is used. You may come across counselors or doctors who diagnose children with adjustment disorder after a stressful event, but if the symptoms persist beyond six months, then the diagnosis is changed to depression. This is normal and appropriate for diagnosis but will not significantly impact the therapy regimen. There is a fine line between adjustment to stressors and depression. When the symptoms last longer than six months and the diagnosis of depression is made, it has been considered reactive depression (depression associated with something external to the person such as a stressful event or experience). In fact, one could argue that in cases when there is a depressivelike response to a stressor, the only difference between adjustment disorder and depression is the length of time one experiences the symptoms.

This is an important issue to remember as we begin to better understand the causes of depression discussed in chapter 3. The term *reactive depression* is typically no longer used as it has been discovered that most long-standing depressive cycles started with a stressful event, just as Kraeplin noticed. The combination of biological predisposition (termed *diathesis*) and the occurrence of stressors, including poor parenting or major stressful events, cause depression. Therefore, it is not helpful to use the term *reactive depression*—most depression starts as a reaction to a stressor in a person predisposed to experience a depressive pattern of responding to stress.

DIATHESIS-STRESS: A FRAMEWORK FOR DEPRESSION AND ITS TREATMENT

In the diathesis-stress model, emotional problems emerge because a person has a physiological and biological vulnerability accompanied by the introduction of environmental stressors that affect the vulnerability. This is analogous to scoring a piece of wood with a starter cut and then bending the wood until it breaks. It will break at the point that was weakened by the score. In psychological terms, an individual has a genetic and biological propensity to become depressed, and in the face of stressful events he or she exhibits symptoms of depression.

Peter Whybrow conducted some of the earliest research on the diathesis-stress model of depression. His diathesis-stress theory of depression was a biobehavioral model, and it included genetic vulnerability, temperament, age, gender, lack of development of proper attachment in childhood, and different personality styles as predisposing factors for depression. He then theorized that there are several elements that precipitate or provoke the depression response in vulnerable individuals. Precipitators include loss of an attachment, loss of social support, loss of control, and multiple stressful life events. Some combination of these stressors and the individual's predisposition were theorized to alter the central nervous system and to affect the neurological systems associated with arousal, mood, motivation, and psychomotor functions. The diathesis-stress model of depression has been further refined and is described in chapter 3 under the heading of Developmental Models of Depression.

As you begin to digest information on depression, it is useful to think about the diathesis-stress model. The causes and treatments of depression are associated with these two aspects of human functioning.

Diathesis

A diathesis is the biological, neurological, and genetic predisposition toward depression. To prevent or treat depression we must be able to intervene on the diathesis in an effort to reduce its influence in response to stress. In the following chapters you will learn that to prevent depression in terms of diathesis, a child must correctly master early developmental tasks to reduce the biological influence of depression throughout the life span. Treatment with medication can correct the biological breakdown that occurs once a child becomes depressed.

Stressors

Stressors are the environmental events that activate the depressive disorder. To prevent or treat depression, we must moderate the stressors that cause the initial depressive episode and provide individuals with the skills necessary to cope with stress. Specifically, to prevent depression we must correct problems that occurred during the first two years of life, allowing children to feel secure about themselves, modulate their emotional reactions to stress, be empathetic toward others, and experience the full range of emotions in a socially appropriate manner. To treat depression, we must instill behavioral and cognitive coping mechanisms and teach children how and when to use them to mitigate the influence of stress. In severe cases, we must also teach the person to live with depression.

CHAPTER 2

3 1208 00200 3657

DIAGNOSIS OF DEPRESSION

There are several types of depression. Some are defined by the *Diagnostic and Statistical Manual of Mental Disorders, Fourth Edition (DSM-IV)* (the book that describes the symptoms of various mental health problems). The types of depression described in the *DSM-IV* are major depression, dysthymia, cyclothymia, and bipolar disorder. These disorders are listed under the heading of Mood Disorders. Other types of depression are reported by psychologists and psychiatrists researching depression but are not listed in the *DSM-IV*. These types of depression include exogenous depression, psychotic depression, agitated depression, double depression, and negative affectivity (these will be discussed later).

DEPRESSION DIAGNOSES OF THE *DSM-IV*

There are basically two types of episodes or phases a child or adolescent with a mood disorder can experience. One is called a depressive episode. This is included in all four types of depression listed in the *DSM-IV;* that is, to be diagnosed with a mood disorder a person must experience some episode or time period of depressed mood or loss of interest in pleasure. The other type of phase is called a manic episode and is only experienced by people diagnosed with the mood disorders cyclothymia or bipolar disorder. In cyclothymia and bipolar disorder, a person experiences episodes of depressed mood at certain times and episodes of abnormally elevated mood at others.

A set of symptoms is typically seen in people experiencing a depressive episode, and another set of symptoms is seen in people experiencing a manic episode. A symptom indicates the presence of a disorder. For these two manifestations, symptoms can be categorized as problems with thoughts, problems with feelings, problems with behaviors, and problems with physiology (sometimes called vegetative or somatic symptoms). Each of the specific symptoms of a depressive or manic episode will be described for each category. It is useful to think of the symptoms of depression in terms of categories because the different treatments of depression tend to target each set of symptoms and their causes.

For symptoms to be of clinical significance, there should be a change in a person's thoughts, feelings, behavior, or physiology, and it should be experienced for a significant period of time, such as two weeks. Also, a single symptom does not represent a diagnosis, nor is it necessary for a person to have every symptom to be depressed. In fact, in the *DSM-IV* there are specific rules that indicate how many symptoms in each category must be present to make a diagnosis. On the other hand, a single symptom may be a sign of a serious problem and should not be categorically ignored. If a child shows a significant change in one or more areas that results in some impairment of functioning, it is a good idea to have her evaluated. This complexity is just one reason that a professional should be consulted to make the diagnosis of depression.

Depressive Episode Symptoms

Problems with Thoughts

Children with depression often experience problems with their thoughts. This is an important aspect of depression; some of the most influential theories of depression such as Aaron Beck's cognitive theory of depression, Martin Seligman's theory of learned helplessness, and Albert Ellis's rational-emotive theory of depression are related to problems with the content of one's thoughts. These theories are described in the chapters on causes and treatment of depression.

It is important to point out that what a depressed person thinks is from his own perspective and may not be grounded in reality. This is known as the subjective or phenomenological nature of thoughts. For example, a child may view herself as a failure academically for missing a single problem on a math test, even though she is earning an A in mathematics. In these types of cases, it is often difficult to get the child to focus on the positive aspect of her math performance rather than the negative. So, although it is not true that the child is incompetent at math, subjectively the child believes she is indeed a failure.

One problem with thoughts has to do with feelings of worthlessness. In this case, a child may say she does not deserve to have friends or to be happy. A child may think she is unworthy of winning, accepting awards, or passing classes. Children in a depressive phase sometimes experience excessive guilt. They inappropriately accept responsibility for the problems of others. In severe cases, a child may overtly express guilt about things wholly unrelated to her. For example, a child's mother may drop something and the child will apologize, indicating that it was her fault. Along with guilt, these children experience shame about themselves. They may be ashamed about the way they look, walk, talk, or smile. They are highly self-critical and look for any opportunity to point out how bad they are. Often, feelings of worthlessness result in an overemphasis on certain physical features. Pimples seem worse than they really are or a nose may seem like Cyrano de Bergerac's.

Another problem with thoughts that is seen during depressive episodes is a diminished ability to think or concentrate. A child with this problem may not be able to do homework as long as he used to, or will be less competent or interested in making decisions for himself. Sometimes children have difficulty concentrating or understanding what is being taught in school. Other problems are thoughts of death and suicide. The latter are called *suicidal ideations* and do not necessarily need to include a plan for suicide. Some children think about wanting to die, while others think specifically about how they would kill themselves. This symptom is covered in more detail in chapter 6.

Problems with Feelings

The hallmark symptom of a depressive episode is depressed mood nearly every day; that is, individuals may say they feel down, sad, or blue, or they may appear sad, tearful, or down most of the time. This includes a sad facial expression or little change in one's emotions. A child's emotions may be resistant to change even when happy events or successes take place. In the diagnostic criteria of the *DSM-IV,* irritability may be used in place of depressed mood to meet the diagnosis.

The next symptom is diminished interest in pleasurable activities. A child will say he does not feel like doing things he typically really enjoyed. Also, the child may feel that she does not deserve pleasure or will appear not to seek pleasure in a variety of situations.

Problems with Behavior

During a depressive phase, an individual may exhibit psychomotor agitation or psychomotor retardation. Psychomotor agitation is when a person is restless, always on the go, and/or fidgety. Psychomotor retardation is the classic lethargic, unmotivated, and passive way of acting that is associated with depression. This is one of those symptoms that covers both ends of the spectrum. Depressed individuals do not all have the same set of symptoms, and this is a perfect example. A depressed person may be agitated during a depressive phase or may be lethargic. Both adversely affect a person's adaptive functioning.

Problems with Physiology

There are several basic physiological processes that may be disturbed in those with depression. These symptoms are often referred to as vegetative because they relate to basic bodily functions. Vegetative symptoms typically appear at one end of the scale. The disruption of basic physiological processes lends support to the notion that depression is partly biological and not simply environmentally induced.

In the depressive phase, a child may experience significant weight loss in the absence of dieting, or significant weight gain. This manifests as a sustained increase or decrease in appetite. In young children, failure to make expected developmental weight gains is also considered a symptom. The next physiological symptoms are insomnia or hypersomnia nearly every day. Children with insomnia complain of not being able to fall asleep, of frequent waking throughout the night, or of waking up very early and not being able to go back to sleep. Hypersomnia is excessive sleep throughout the night or excessive sleeping during the day after a normal night's sleep. Another physiological symptom of a depressive episode is fatigue and a lack of energy. Chronic fatigue can present as complaints of being tired, not feeling motivated, or having various diffuse physical pains and discomforts.

Manic Episode Symptoms

Problems with Thoughts

During a manic episode, children may experience two thought problems: racing thoughts or flight of ideas. Racing thoughts are manifested by rapidly changing topics of discussion or an inability to finish a complete thought. A more severe case of racing thoughts is called flight of ideas. Here children will exhibit a near-continuous flow of speech that rapidly jumps from topic to topic. Usually the associations are understandable or based on rhyming, but they are obviously not normal. Flight of ideas should be considered a very serious symptom requiring immediate action. Another thought symptom observed during a manic episode is distractibility. A child will have a very hard time focusing his attention on one thing and will be pulled off task easily and frequently. This symptom is easily confused with the distractibility found in attention-deficit/hyperactivity disorder (ADHD). The difference is that in depression, distractibility occurs only during the manic episode, while in ADHD it is seen relatively consistently from early in the child's development.

Problems with Feelings

Problems with feelings during a manic episode include inflated self-esteem or grandiosity. During these episodes a child may feel particularly invincible or prone to exaggerate his abilities. This is not simply the return to normal self-esteem after the remission of a depressive phase; rather, the child may make outrageous claims about her popularity or athletic abilities in the face of substantial contradictory evidence. Although this symptom is sometimes difficult to detect, a good clinician can readily sense when a child is experiencing this level of grandiosity.

Problems with Behavior

In manic episodes, there are a variety of problem behaviors. A child may become extremely talkative and may have a hard time being quiet. He acts as though there is some pressure to keep talking, almost as if something bad might happen if he stopped. Another symptom is increased activity toward a specific goal. The child cannot stop working on a specific task or seems obsessed about some aspect of an activity. This symptom can also manifest as psychomotor agitation. The third behavioral symptom is excessive involvement in pleasurable activities that may be harmful. In children, this includes foolishly spending all their money, seeking relationships with peers who resist their friendship, and other impulsive acts.

Problems with Physiology

The physiological symptom experienced during a manic episode is reduced need for sleep. This symptom is only at one end of the spectrum but correlates with the balance of manic episode symptoms in that the person has substantial energy and is very active. Despite the talkativeness and overactivity, these children report feeling rested after very little sleep each night.

Major Depression

For the diagnosis of depression, a child must experience five of the symptoms of a depressive episode for two or more weeks. Further, he must have either a depressed mood or loss of interest in pleasure. In the case of children, depressed mood can be replaced by irritability. Irritability is used in the diagnosis of children because they experience more physical complaints, ill temper, and social withdrawal than adults.

Melanie is a sixteen-year-old high school student. She lives with her natural parents and older brother. She spoke regularly with her school guidance counselor, with whom she had a trusting relationship. One day she came into the counselor's office claiming she had attempted to cut her wrist with a knife the night before. She said she wanted to die, but it would hurt too much to cut herself, and she was afraid of pain. Melanie had superficial cuts on one wrist but said she was still suicidal and was planning to overdose on some pills from a friend. The counselor felt that this was all quite unexpected and called in the school psychologist to help with the situation. Melanie had some signs of depression prior to this incident, but they were subtle. Her emotions were a little flatter than usual, but Melanie attributed this to stress over school work. She did not want to reveal her true feelings because she was embarrassed and did not really know what to do. She was confused about her friendships, sleeping much more than usual, not eating, and she could not concentrate in class. She complained of being gloomy and sluggish during the day and said she could not face another day of the problems she was having with her friends but wanted it all to go away.

The psychologist and counselor faced their biggest challenge—telling Melanie that they would have to call her mother. Melanie was upset by this and pleaded for them not to call her parents. She said that her mother would not care, that she was busy at work, and then promised she would not hurt herself if they just did not call. This was a difficult decision for the professionals because notifying the parents of something relayed in confidence might undermine the trust they had established with the student. On the other hand, they had a duty to ensure the safety of the child and thus had to notify the parents.

To Melanie's surprise, her mother dropped everything and came right to the school. When she arrived she hugged her daughter and asked what was wrong. Her mother had noticed a change in Melanie, but did not know what to make of it. She was shocked to discover how drastic her daughter was acting. Although initially resentful, Melanie listened to her mother and agreed to treatment. The family was fortunate enough to have good insurance coverage, and Melanie was hospitalized for three days and started on antidepressant medication. She was discharged with an extensive aftercare plan that included individual and family counseling, medication monitoring, and instructions on what to do if she felt suicidal again. On returning to school, Melanie resumed her contact with the counselor and was thankful that she had notified her mother.

Dysthymic Disorder

Dysthymic disorder is a different form of depression, but not necessarily less devastating. To be diagnosed with dysthymia a child must experience a depressed mood or irritability for one year. This is different than the adult criteria that require a depressed mood for two years. In addition to depressed mood or irritability, the child must experience two or more of the following symptoms: poor appetite or overeating, insomnia or hypersomnia, low energy or fatigue, low self-esteem, poor concentration or difficulty making decisions, or feelings of hopelessness. Dysthymic disorder is more chronic than major depression, but the individual tends to show less symptoms.

Joe is a ten-year-old boy who had been referred to counseling for disruptive behavior at school. His mother is a drug addict and his father is a migrant worker in a rural community. Joe's parents never married. Until the age of three Joe lived with his mother. Currently he is living with his paternal grandparents who have raised him since then. He has been in therapy many times over the last three years. He is described as irritable, quick-tempered, and hypersensitive to criticism. Teachers have difficulty getting him to pay attention to any tasks he anticipates he cannot do, and he is failing all of his classes. He loves reading, but teachers complain that he will begin reading and then refuse to transition to other academic tasks. He has been sent out of class a number of times for non-compliance.

Joe did not believe he had any problems but did admit that he has been sad. When questioned about these feelings, he cannot say what he is sad about. When asked about his parents, he tends to overidealize them and denies that his relationship with them is different from any other child's. He frequently indicates that when his mother gets some money he is going to live with her again. His grandparents say that his mother has no intention of taking him back and that he has developed this fantasy. He is taking the antidepressant Paxil, prescribed by his family physician, and had been doing so for eight months prior to being referred to counseling. Joe reported that the most important thing in his life is his father's dog who lives with him. A year prior to treatment, his symptoms were exacerbated by the death of his paternal uncle. This uncle was particularly fond of Joe and remained close to him until the time of his death. Recently, when his dog got sick Joe started to talk about his uncle in therapy.

Since Joe has experienced several losses in his short life, including the death of his uncle and the separation loss of both parents, his treatment focused on correcting problems with attachment. He enjoyed playing games, and this was used to engage Joe and help him build a relationship with the therapist. One issue that the therapist considered is whether Joe's oppositional behavior is a way of testing his grandparents to see if they will abandon him as well. Since Joe was willing to talk about his dog, this served as a metaphor and a stepping stone to talking about attachment and loss issues. Treatment also focused on developing a sense of closure, particularly with regard to his parents' abandonment.

Bipolar Disorder

There are two varieties of bipolar disorder, called *bipolar I* and *bipolar II*. Bipolar disorder used to be called *manic depression* because of the cycling that occurs between episodes of depression and mania. These cycles have been further classified into subcategories (these are beyond the scope of this book). For bipolar I to be diagnosed, three of the symptoms of a manic episode described above must be present for a period of at least one week. The child's mood must be abnormally and persistently elevated, expansive, or irritable for the same period of time. Technically, one does not have to ever have had a depressive episode to meet the criteria for bipolar I; however, in children this is rarely the case. Typically, children have experienced several major depressive episodes prior to experiencing their first manic episode.

For the diagnosis of bipolar II, a person does not have a "full-blown" manic episode; rather, he experiences a hypomanic episode. A hypomanic episode is characterized by an elevated, expansive, or irritable mood lasting four days, but symptoms are not as extreme as in a manic episode. Along with the mood disturbance, the child will also experience three or more of the symptoms of a manic episode described above. Unlike bipolar I, there must be a history of or the presence of a major depressive episode. As we discussed earlier, this is moot because children typically experience depressive episodes first.

Jim was referred for counseling by his psychiatrist. He was seen the week after he was discharged from the hospital. He is fifteen years old and six-and-a-half feet tall. His parents are divorced, and he is currently living with his mother. His mother has a history of bipolar disorder and is taking the prescription drug lithium carbonate as treatment. His father lives out of town and visits Jim periodically. His father has no history of mental illness. Jim has a background of fighting with his younger sibling and is very protective of his mother.

This is the event that led to his hospitalization: One morning he did not say good-bye to his mom when he left for school (unusual for him). The family found him in the backyard standing in the pool with his head barely above water, fully clothed, with his mother's dress over him. He had been in the water for at least thirty minutes, apparently in some psychotic state. He had been exhibiting grandiose thinking just prior to this, stating he was a fabulous artist and was working for the government to create a new generation of colorful money. He exhibited excessive levels of energy; he would stay up all night working on projects. When Jim was hospitalized he was initially prescribed the antipsychotic medication Risperdal and lithium carbonate. Risperdal was decreased during the hospitalization and finally discontinued.

Prior to being hospitalized he failed all of his classes at school. He had no friends. He had always had trouble developing and maintaining relationships. He reports that he yearns for friends, but tends to isolate himself. He says he used to call friends, but only occasionally would they visit him. In retrospect, Jim indicated that he has probably had many depressive episodes. For example, a girl he hoped to date started dating another boy. This was devastating to him, and he remembered feeling like he was "dead" for several weeks.

Jim liked drawing, which he is not very good at, and playing video games. The first goal of therapy was to get him to comply with medication treatment; he finally agreed begrudgingly to voluntarily take his medication orally to avoid being given injections. Jim attended weekly counseling sessions for five months. Some of the sessions were with Jim individually and some included his mother and brother. Jim began disclosing his feelings in therapy and indicated that he gets very mad when his mother goes out on dates. One man his mother dated was emotionally abusive to Jim as well as his mom. At one point, this man became physically abusive toward Jim. On reflection, Jim realized that he chose to take the abuse to protect his younger brother and mother. He believed that if he took the beatings this man would not beat up the other family members. Jim was tremendously angry and traumatized by this and would not refer to the man by name. At this point in therapy, he expressed his anger and sadness and sobbed throughout sessions. He described the pool incident as when "he snapped." This was a relatively discrete event for him. He had insight into his history of depressive episodes, but he did not recognize the developing manic episode that resulted in his hospitalization. As part of therapy he was taught to identify the signs of depressive and manic episodes. He requested to discontinue treatment, and this was agreed on because it gave him control over his life; it was felt there was a better chance of him coming back to therapy when he needed it. Although treatment progress was slow, he did show an increase in school achievement and made passing grades in a few classes. Jim did not achieve to his intellectual ability, however. He became more socially assertive and began asking friends over and talking to girls. Treatment was discontinued with the understanding that he would continue his medications and return as needed.

Cyclothymic Disorder

As the name suggests, cyclothymic disorder includes periods of elevated mood that cycle with periods of depressed mood. Specifically, children diagnosed with cyclothymia experience numerous hypo-manic episodes and numerous depressive episodes that do not meet the criteria for major depression (such as seen in dysthymic disor-der). For children, this pattern must occur for at least one year. This is different than the criteria for adults, in which this pattern occurs for a period of at least two years.

Kenny is an eleven-year-old boy whose school placement is a self-contained classroom for children with emotional prob-lems. He experiences periods lasting for three to four days in which he is overactive, disruptive, and talkative. During these days, teachers have a difficult time working with Kenny, who often has to be removed from his physical education class due to lack of self-control. Kenny also experiences periods of obvious depressed affect (emotional expressions) and is much more lethargic and unmotivated, sometimes lasting a week or more. He lives in a therapeutic group home for children with emotional problems who are in the custody of the state.

Kenny comes to school on a special education bus because, at times, he can be extremely disruptive on a regular bus. The special education bus transports only five children, along with a driver and an assistant, and is the same size as a regular bus. The special education teachers meet the bus every morning, and when Kenny arrives, they can tell whether he is in an ele-vated or depressed mood. He has periods of relatively nor-mal moods, during which he behaves appropriately and is a pleasure to be around. Kenny has incredible resilience when interacting with his peers. He may offend them terribly one day and then ignore them completely the next day. During his normal days, however, he will approach them, initiate appro-priate conversation, and play as if nothing happened before.

This probably has to do with the nature of his world, and out of necessity, he must experience every day as a new day and repress the past to cope.

Additional Diagnostic Criteria

The disorders defined in the *DSM-IV* are characterized by sets of symptoms. In addition to these symptoms, other criteria must be met and other diagnoses must be ruled out. The diagnosis of depression is not as simple as counting symptoms, and it requires the expertise of a trained clinician. Of these other criteria, one often not considered by the layperson is that the symptoms must result in significant distress or impairment of social, occupational, or other important areas of functioning. For children, this means impairment of school and/or social functioning. Adolescents may also experience impairment of occupational functioning.

OTHER FORMS OF DEPRESSION

The types of depression just described are the most rigorously researched and universally accepted forms of depression. They are important not only for research and consistent classification; they are typically used for filing insurance reimbursements for treatment. There are other forms of depression reported by clinicians and researchers. Many clinicians do not hesitate to use terms other than those listed in the *DSM-IV* because they may not have to worry about reimbursements or they feel these other descriptions are more meaningful for treatment.

Endogenous Versus Exogenous Depression

Endogenous means the depression is caused by something "inside" the person or by a biological cause. Typically, there is no significant antecedent event triggering the onset of an endogenous depressive episode. Endogenous depression is associated with primarily physiological symptoms such as sleep problems, changes in appetite, and fatigue. The probability of having multiple episodes is theoretically higher because of the strong biological component. On the other hand, *exogenous* means the depression is caused by something "outside" the person. Exogenous depression is primarily caused by external events such as major losses, public humiliation, or chronic difficulties in coping with stress. Exogenous depression is sometimes called reactive or situational depression. Exogenous depression is associated with more thinking and feeling symptoms, including feelings of worthlessness, hopelessness, and inability to concentrate.

Exogenous depression and endogenous depression are not mutually exclusive. If a child has endogenous depression, there still may exist environmental triggers for its onset. This distinction between endogenous and exogenous is therefore somewhat artificial. As with the diathesis-stress model introduced in chapter 1, there is almost always an interaction between the environment and a person's biology for the onset of depression. Thus, the description of depression as either endogenous or exogenous just reflects the most salient aspect in the eyes of the clinician. Despite the intuitive appeal of the description of exogenous depression, there is little research to support that it is truly independent or different from endogenous depression. Findings such as this lend substantial support to the notion of diathesis-stress as the cause of depression.

Psychotic Versus Neurotic Depression

In some cases of severe depression, and more frequently in bipolar disorder, a child may experience what are referred to as psychotic symptoms that include hallucinations or delusions. Hallucinations are false sensory perceptions, such as hearing things others do not hear or seeing things others do not see. Delusions are fixed false beliefs, such as believing that someone is out to get you or that you are being monitored by electronic devices. These are also symptoms of schizophrenia. When depression is the primary diagnosis, however, and psychotic symptoms emerge, the episode is described as psychotic depression. In *DSM-IV* terminology, the episode would be called major depression with psychotic features or bipolar I disorder with psychotic features. Neurotic depression, on the other hand, is synonymous with reactive depression, exogenous depression, or mild depression. As with exogenous depression, the term *neurotic depression* has little usefulness in describing a specific type of depression.

Agitated Versus Retarded Depression

The distinction between agitated and retarded depression is useful as it describes two different clusters of symptoms a child may experience. Agitated depression includes an irritable mood, sleeplessness, lack of appetite, and psychomotor agitation. Clinically, agitated depression is associated with risk taking and, in adolescents, promiscuity, excessive partying, and sensation seeking. Agitated depression can easily be overlooked, and the behaviors associated with it sometimes are described as typical of adolescence. It is a serious form of depression, however, and can lead to bad outcomes such as teen pregnancy, motor vehicle accidents, and drug addiction.

Retarded depression is the constellation of symptoms typically thought of as depression. The symptoms include hypersomnia, overeating, fatigue, lack of motivation, and a lack of pleasure seeking. The distinction between agitated and retarded depression has implications for medication treatment. Specifically, if agitated depression is primary, then the medication should help slow down the person and reduce his agitation. In cases of retarded depression, the medication should get the person on her feet and provide some energy.

Double Depression

Double depression occurs when a child with a diagnosis of dysthymic disorder experiences a major depressive episode. After the major depressive episode has passed, the child returns to a state of dysthymia.

Negative Affectivity

Negative affectivity is a type of depression that includes symptoms of both depression and anxiety. I believe this pattern is seen in children because their diathesis or biological vulnerability in response to stress has not fully differentiated. Typically, negative affectivity will differentiate as the child matures into adulthood and will become either primarily depression or primarily anxiety. Negative affectivity is characterized by depressed mood or irritability, feelings of worthlessness, chronic worry, unrealistic self-appraisal, and

Developmental Listing of Depression Symptoms

Infants	• Unresponsive when talked to or touched, never smile or cry, or may cry often and be difficult to soothe • Failure to gain weight (not due to other medical illness) • Unmotivated in play • Problems with eating or sleeping • Digestive disorders (constipation/diarrhea) • Restless, oversensitive to noise or touch
Children	• Persistent unhappiness, negativity, complaining, chronic boredom, no initiative • Frequent disobedience • Easily frustrated, frequent crying, low self-esteem, overly sensitive • Inability to pay attention, remember, or make decisions, easily distracted, mind goes blank • Eating or sleeping problems • Bed-wetting, constipation, diarrhea, impulsiveness, accident prone • Chronic worry and fear • Extreme self-consciousness • Slowed speech and body movements • Physical symptoms such as dizziness, headaches, stomachaches, arm or leg aches, nail biting (not due to other medical causes) • Suicidal thoughts or attempts
Adolescents	• Physical symptoms such as dizziness, headaches, stomachaches, arm or leg aches due to muscle tension, digestive disorders (not due to other medical causes) • Persistent unhappiness, negativity, irritability • Uncontrollable anger or outbursts of rage • Overly self-critical, unwarranted guilt, low self-esteem

Adolescents *continued*	• Inability to concentrate, think straight, remember, or make decisions • Slowed or hesitant speech or body movements • Loss of interest in once pleasurable activities • Low energy, chronic fatigue, sluggishness • Change in appetite, noticeable weight loss or weight gain, abnormal eating patterns • Chronic worry, excessive fear • Preoccupation with death themes in literature, music, drawings, speaking of death repeatedly, fascination with guns/knives • Suicidal thoughts, plans, or attempts

a generally negative view of the world and the future. In my experience, children with negative affectivity have been subjected to overly critical parenting and relatively constant demeaning messages from caregivers.

ASSESSMENT OF DEPRESSION

At this point, we have discussed the many forms of childhood depression and described the symptoms commonly associated with each. How does the clinician go about determining if your child is experiencing depression and, if so, its type? This is the topic of the following discussion. Diagnosing the particular type of depression has important implications for treatment planning. You may argue that the type of depression a person has does not matter; rather, what truly matters are the causes of a person's specific pattern of symptoms. This is basically what the clinician is doing when making a diagnosis. Diagnoses are just summary statements for a pattern of behavior. Particularly for talking therapy treatment of depression, the clinician will actively try to determine the causes of a person's symptom pattern during the assessment. In purely pharmacological treatment models, however, the cause has less importance than the pattern or topography of the disorder. The following discussion provides a typical method of assessment to ascertain both the pattern of symptoms and the diagnosis and to give some ideas about the causes of the depression.

Questionnaires

When you and your child arrive at the clinician's office, the first step is usually filling out a stack of paperwork. Other than the insurance forms, the questionnaires are an important part of the assessment process. Typically, you will be asked about your child's developmental and medical history. There should be a wide variety of questions about family members, history of mental illness in the family, mental health treatment history, and possible stressors. These factors are important to the assessment of depression because they indicate biological and environmental causes. Further, family history of mental illness is particularly important; depression is frequently passed genetically among family members.

Another set of questionnaires you may fill out asks many true-false or rating scale–type questions about your child. Typical scales used are the *Personality Inventory for Children,* the *Achenbach Child Behavior Checklist,* and the *Behavior Assessment System for Children.* These questionnaires are designed to give a "broad-band" picture of your child's personality and emotional functioning. Broad-band means the questionnaires pick up a variety of types of emotional functioning, including depression. Other areas assessed are anxiety, thought disorder, aggressiveness, social problems, leadership, and school functioning. Because the questionnaires are broad-band instruments, some of the questions may not appear relevant to your child, but it is important to complete all questions as accurately as possible because the clinician uses the scores on different areas of functioning to help understand your child's overall personality.

Some clinicians may ask your child's teachers to complete similar questionnaires. There are teacher versions of most questionnaires that measure the same types of emotional functioning as the parent versions. Teachers are typically familiar with completing these questionnaires for school counselors and school psychologists. The teacher's view is important to determine how your child is functioning in his different environments. Does he act the same way at school as at home? Also, part of the diagnosis is determining if the emotional symptoms interfere with your child's daily functioning.

Your child may also be asked to fill out similar questionnaires. If your child is eight or older, she can fill out broad-band questionnaires such as the *Behavior Assessment System for Children.* Older children may complete questionnaires with hundreds of questions, such as the *Minnesota Multiphasic Personality Inventory-Adolescent.* There are also narrow-band scales your child may fill out. These are questionnaires with fewer questions that assess only one area of emotional functioning. For example, the *Children's Depression Inventory* is a very popular test for identifying depression in children. Of increasing importance are measures of emotional intelligence that assess a child's empathy skills, social skills, and social problem solving. There are many good questionnaires available for parents, teachers, and children, and there are new ones being developed every day. Questionnaires represent an important method of standardized assessment, and those who complete them should do so as accurately as possible.

Clinical Interview

The next source of information for making the diagnosis of depression is the clinical interview. At this point you or you and your child will meet with the clinician who will ask you a variety of questions. Many of these questions are quite personal and can be uncomfortable. Good clinicians will help make you and your child comfortable, but if there is something you are not ready to disclose, then save it for a later session. During the clinical interview the clinician is looking to clarify what was reported on the questionnaires and will ask relevant follow-up questions. At this time the clinician is also assessing your child's mental status. Mental status includes alertness, orientation to time and place, physical appearance, speech, and other aspects of functioning. The clinical interview is a good time to ask any questions and to allay any concerns you may have.

Formal Testing

During the evaluation session, your child may be given individual tests of personality, intelligence, academic achievement, or neuropsychological functioning. If your child completed questionnaires, these certainly qualify as formal tests; however, in this section I refer to tests given to your child by the clinician or his assistant. There are a variety of individually administered personality tests you may expect. Your child may be given the *Rorschach Psychodiagnostic Test,* also known as the inkblot test. This is known as a projective test because it does not directly ask questions about depression or anxiety; rather, responses to the test are interpreted by the clinician. The *Rorschach* takes a considerable amount of skill and training to administer and interpret, but it is one of the most widely used personality tests in the world. Another projective test is the *Thematic Apperception Test.* In this test the child is shown pictures and asked to tell stories about them. Again, this test is subject to high levels of interpretation by the clinician, but it can be very useful in understanding how your child views himself in relation to others and the world around him. The sentence completion test is another more directive test of personality subject to high-level interpretation.

Another form of projective assessment looks at the play in which your child engages. The clinician may ask your child to draw pictures, play with clay, or play with different toys. Play-based assessment can be interpreted from a number of different theoretical perspectives, but the gist is that the child's thoughts and feelings are acted out in her drawings and play. This is a particularly useful technique to use with small children who do not respond well to more structured assessment methods or direct questioning.

Intelligence tests can be given to children as young as six months of age and to adults as old as a hundred years. Intelligence is quite stable over the life span and can be very accurately assessed when a child is only five or six years old. Intelligence may be included in a "comprehensive" assessment of your child for a number of reasons. Intelligence is used to make other diagnoses, which may help to explain academic failure. For example, learning disabilities, borderline intelligence, or traumatic brain injury may account for your child's academic difficulties; thus, intelligence testing helps to find or rule out other problems. Also, styles of intellectual functioning can help explain a child's strengths and weaknesses that are important to treatment planning. For example, some children may be very verbally oriented while others may be more perceptually oriented or "hands on." Intelligence tests are individually administered and usually take about an hour to give. The child is asked to solve a wide variety of problems using words, spatial relations, and inductive and deductive reasoning. Typical intelligence tests are the *Wechsler Intelligence Scale for Children* and the *Differential Abilities Scale.*

Academic achievement tests are given as part of a comprehensive evaluation to determine your child's level of reading, writing, and mathematics skills. Achievement scores are important in making other diagnoses that may account for academic problems and frustration such as learning disabilities and traumatic brain injury. Academic achievement tests are administered individually and include tests of sight word reading, paragraph comprehension, applied mathematics, computational mathematics, spelling, and paragraph composition. Typical achievement tests include the *Wechsler Individual Achievement Test* and the *Woodcock-Johnson Tests of Achievement.*

In cases of suspected head injury, chronic illness, neonatal injury, or seizures that may be related to a depressive episode, neuropsychological testing may be indicated. Neuropsychological tests are designed to measure brain-behavior relationships that are disrupted by different types of trauma to the brain. Specifically, these tests measure attention, concentration, organization, planning, reasoning, speed of mental processing, and memory. These are all areas of cognitive functioning. In addition, head trauma can result in changes in personality, including the onset of depression. Although not the focus of this book, it is important to recognize that depression may result as a response to head injury or other neurological problems.

Assessment Report

After completing the evaluation, the clinician will have a reporting session in which the test results are summarized, a diagnosis is made, and a treatment plan is decided on. In some cases, you may receive a written report that is also covered in a face-to-face session with the clinician. In cases of comprehensive evaluations, you must receive a complete report detailing the history taken, tests given, test results, interpretations of all clinical data, diagnostic impressions, and recommendations. This is important if the school is involved in treatment (see chapter 7), if you take your child to another clinician, or if there is a relapse several years later.

Developing a Treatment Plan

The final step in a psychological evaluation is to develop a treatment plan. I have seen many patients who had been treated by other clinicians and did not know what their treatment plan was or even what they were working on in therapy. Be clear on what the specific problems are and what exactly is being treated. A treatment plan should include a description of the behavior or problem defined by the evaluation results; that is, what are the specific aspects of the child's behavior that are targeted for treatment? For example, if your child experiences feelings of worthlessness, the description of the behavior should include the exact types of thoughts and feelings the child has. After describing the behaviors, specific goals should be set. In this example, the goal may be to increase the child's ability to notice her positive attributes and express them verbally twice per day.

CHAPTER 3

THEORIES OF DEPRESSION

In the last chapter we discussed what depression looks like or how it presents itself in behavior. Further, we discussed what a clinician does to determine if a child is depressed. This chapter is concerned with theories that attempt to explain or predict depression. What causes depression, and why do some people get depressed and not others? These models or theories are what the clinician uses to interpret the data gathered during the evaluation. By understanding the causes of childhood depression, therapists are able to effectively treat the child. On a broader scale, theories of depression are also important because they point to what needs to be changed in society and in families to prevent the occurrence of depression. Depression is a widespread problem, and anything a parent can do to mitigate its onset or severity is worthwhile. These topics are discussed in chapter 8.

There are several theories of depression. Each accounts for some of the types of depression we have discussed. Because people are complex, more than one theory may account for a specific child's depression. As you read this chapter and its different theories of depression, think about your child and consider the degree to which any or all of the theories match or are relevant to your child. We will examine various ways of understanding childhood depression, including developmental, behavioral, cognitive, and biological aspects. We will also examine the diathesis-stress model of childhood depression, which integrates many of the ideas discussed in other theories and provides a good general framework and organizing model for understanding the causes and treatment of depression.

DEVELOPMENTAL MODELS OF DEPRESSION

Developmental models of depression are concerned with what happens during a child's developmental period that may cause the child to become depressed. This idea that early events determine later personality functioning is not new. At the turn of the twentieth century, Sigmund Freud asserted that a child's personality was largely developed by the end of his or her fifth year. Freud believed how a child learned to adjust to early experiences defined a child's later personality. For example, a child may learn to control his own emotions and the world around him through the use of defense mechanisms developed in early childhood. These defense mechanisms, once found to be effective, are then elaborated and honed. Freud believed that the basic structure or foundation of personality was established very early in life and that after age five any changes were elaboration on this early personality foundation. Freud believed that depression was the result of poor resolution of the conflict between primitive urges (id) and internalization or acceptance of social taboos against the expression of these urges (superego).

Freud, and the therapists that adhered to his theory (referred to as psychoanalysis), did not believe that children could experience depression as we know it because children, by virtue of their age, could not develop a superego sufficient to undergo such conflict. By strict adherence to this position, psychoanalytic theorists were left with an understanding of childhood development that failed to account for and denied the now obvious reality that children do become depressed. This postulate has since been revised by those who practice psychoanalysis.

Since the time of Freud and his psychoanalytic adherents, other theories have offered ways of understanding depression in light of a child's development. In particular, there are two primary developmental theories of depression. The first has to do with the attachment or bond between a child and his caregiver; the second is a vastly more comprehensive theory called depressotypic organizations.

Attachment and Depression

Attachment theory asserts that the bond between a child and a caregiver, typically the mother, is central to the child's immediate and long-term adjustment. From birth and particularly during the first few years, the quality of the relationship between baby and mother is crucial. When there is consistent love, safety, and security, the child develops a strong bond with the caregiver. The caregiver provides a secure base from which the child may explore the broader world, knowing that when times are tough and the outside world is threatening, she may return to this emotional safe haven. When this attachment does not develop properly, there is a potential for depression to result.

To understand how attachment development can be disrupted, one must understand how these attachments form. There are several theories on how attachment develops. Freud believed that in the earliest stage of life, the oral stage, which occurs during the child's first year when eating is of primary importance, infants become attached to the person that provides oral satisfaction. The child's primary form of gratification is found through sucking and eating, forming dependence on the object of his oral gratification. During this early stage of life, the child develops intense feelings of dependency because the baby must rely on others completely for care and protection. According to Freudian psychologists, when oral needs are not met satisfactorily, anxiety and insecurity may persist throughout life.

Erik Erikson, a psychoanalytically oriented psychologist, accepted many of Freud's assumptions but also departed from Freud in important ways. Erikson emphasized lifelong development and asserted that at every period of life we are challenged to resolve issues that are critical for our long-term adjustment. According to Erikson, our earliest challenge, which occurs within the first year, is developing the capacity to trust another person in the most fundamental way possible. He believed that the infant child, once offered physical and psychological security, will establish a foundation of trust and will face life with a minimal amount of fear and apprehension about the future. He believed this trust was fostered through responsive and sensitive parenting.

Since Freud, other psychologists have studied attachment. In the 1950s, Harry Harlow conducted a series of ingenious and now-famous studies of attachment using infant rhesus monkeys and "surrogate mothers." In part, Harlow challenged Freud's notion that sucking was central to attachment. To do this, he raised infant monkeys with two types of surrogate mothers. Some of the infant monkeys were raised in cages that had surrogate mothers that were made of wire mesh with a feeding device protruding from them. Other infant monkeys had identical wire-mesh mothers, except Harlow wrapped soft material around the wire, making these surrogate mothers more huggable. What remained consistent for all the monkeys was the potential for oral gratification from the surrogate mothers. In line with his thinking, the baby monkeys preferred to climb on and hug the surrogate mothers that were soft and cuddly. In fact, the monkeys with only the wire surrogate mothers displayed a wide range of behavior difficulties. Since these monkeys were studied over a period of time, Harlow was able to demonstrate that these monkeys had difficulty reintegrating with the family and that their problems were long standing. Harlow challenged Freud's assertion that attachment is primarily related to eating. He asserted that the physical contact associated with comfort contact was the most important variable in attachment. It is interesting to note that this idea of comfort contact is used today in neonatal hospital units for children on respirators. To promote proper attachment, parents come to the hospital daily and hold their children in a rocking chair near the respirator.

Another group of psychologists that made a significant contribution to understanding human behavior is the ethologists. Ethologists study animal behavior in the wild and draw inferences about human behaviors from these observations. Examples of valid ethological contributions to human understanding are the comparison of territoriality of stickleback fish and the territoriality of humans or the spacing of pigeons on a telephone wire and the spacing of humans in a waiting room. The ethologist Konrad Lorenz observed firsthand that ducklings attached to objects at a critical time in their development. He referred to this phenomenon as imprinting. While raising ducks on his farm, Lorenz found himself the unexpected object of several ducklings' attachment. Because he was present at a specific time in their young lives, the ducklings imprinted on Lorenz, following him around the farm in a line, just as they would their actual mothers. From this, ethologists have asserted that the first months of life is a critical period for forming attachments. During these months, the affection and attention of a caregiver are essential for bonding to occur. If consistent loving care is not provided during this critical period, the child will likely develop impaired attachment and assumedly have difficulty with relationships later in life.

Another group of theorists, the object relation theorists, such as John Bowlby, Margaret Mahler, and Mary Ainsworth, have come to understand human attachment by observing the interaction or "dance" between mothers and children firsthand. They assert that, at birth, the infant does not have the cognitive capacity to attach as the newborn's world is a blur and behavior is by and large the result of reflexes. Within the first few weeks, the child begins to develop a bond with the mother as well as a language of coos, babbles, and cries that are universal, yet unique to that particular mother and child. According to these theorists, early on the child does not differentiate between self and others. The infant child does not draw a distinction between herself and the object (mother) that is providing for all her needs. Magically, the baby thinks, I am hungry and I am fed, not knowing that the feeding is the result of the actions of another person. After the first few weeks the child begins to differentiate between self and others, realizing that he is not fused or one in the same as the mother. As the child matures, the sense of self and other becomes more elaborated. The first two years of life are critical for developing a healthy balance between dependence and autonomy. Two examples of the normal but difficult struggle between dependence and autonomy can be observed directly when the child experiences separation anxiety or stranger anxiety. With separation anxiety the child displays exaggerated fear about the actual or anticipated separation from his caregiver. With stranger anxiety the child shows an extreme fear of strangers that is typically calmed by the comfort of the caregiver. One final example of the child negotiating the balance between dependence and autonomy is rapproachment. *Rapproachment* is the familiar case of the child, at about eighteen to twenty-four months, venturing away from her mother, say, into an adjacent room, then racing back to cling to the comfort of her mother. Commonly known as the "terrible twos," the child will demand independence and then demand refuge in seemingly unidentifiable patterns. Rapproachment has also been referred to as *emotional refueling*.

Based on the outcome of the relationship between the child and the caregiver, there are three types of attachment that may emerge. The first is the secure attachment. Here a child moves freely away from the mother, uses the caregiver as a secure base to explore the environment, and responds positively to being picked up by others. Second is the anxious-avoidant attachment. Children with this type of attachment ignore the mother, avoid her gaze, and fail to seek proximity with her. Third is the anxious-resistant attachment, in which the child clings to the mother but at the same time fights closeness, kicks and pushes away the mother, and resists her.

Although these theorists differ regarding the mechanism that causes attachment, all agree that attachment is a primary issue in the first year of life. Further, these theorists agree that the infant child needs a caregiver that provides consistent physical and psychological security. From this bond, the child develops a foundation of trust and confidence that is the base from which future challenges are negotiated. The development of a proper attachment has far-reaching implications and serves to organize emotions, cognitive representations, and behaviors in relation to the quality of the emotional and physical availability of the caregiver.

So what accounts for insecure and resistant attachments? One obvious answer is the primary caregiver. Parents who foster these types of attachments tend not to complete interrupted interactions with their infants; that is, the child is ignored when the parent is offered an opportunity to talk with an adult, meet the needs of a sibling, or make a phone call. There should be closure to infant-parent interactions even if they are briefly interrupted. Also, parents of children with insecure and resistant attachments are less likely to maintain good interactions with their infants. The parent consistently only briefly interacts with the child as needed, and there is little effort to develop consistency in social exchanges. Finally, these parents manifest less coordinated activity with their infants. Secure attachments develop in part through a smooth, almost choreographed interaction between the child and the parent. This final problem, however, is not always the parent's fault. Children are born with a certain temperament, and that can account for a parent and a child not "hitting it off."

Temperament is a behavioral style and characteristic way of responding in infants and toddlers. It is a stable characteristic of newborns that is shaped and modified by the child's later experiences. Temperament becomes more malleable with time.

Researchers suggest that there is a moderate influence of heredity on temperament. What is important about temperament in terms of attachment is the match between the child's nature and the parent's nature. There is a reciprocal interaction between the parent and the child with regard to temperament. Parents influence their infants' temperament, just as infants influence their parents' temperament.

Alexander Thomas and Stella Chess are temperament researchers, and they describe three dimensions of temperament. First is the easy temperament, marked by a generally positive mood. A child with an easy temperament readily establishes regular routines in infancy and adapts easily to new experiences. Second is the difficult temperament, marked by a tendency to react negatively and cry frequently. A child with a difficult temperament does not readily establish regular routines and is slow to adjust to new experiences. Third is the slow-to-warm-up temperament, characterized by low activity level and somewhat negative reactions. These children show a low intensity of mood expression.

Other researchers, Arnold Buss and Robert Plomin, have described different yet important aspects of temperament. First is emotionality, which is a tendency to be distressed in infancy. Emotional responses of distress are fear and anger. Children are labeled "easy" or "difficult" on the basis of their emotionality. Second is sociability, which is the tendency to prefer the company of others and to respond warmly to them. Third is activity level; this relates to the infant's tempo and vigor of movement and may range from highly energetic to tranquil.

There is no right or wrong temperament, though some children's temperament makes parenting easier. What is important to parenting is the development of that early attachment. In cases where the infant's and parent's temperaments are very different, it is incumbent on the parent to recognize these differences and adjust as needed. This is, of course, outside the abilities of the child, but, more important, it is an indication to the child that the parent is doing what is necessary to meet his basic needs.

The next important variable parents must understand during the early developmental period is emotions. Emotions are feelings or affect that involve a mixture of physiological arousal, such as increased heart rate, and overt behavior, such as facial expressions. Emotions are considered the first language between parents and infants. The body and face play an important role in understanding children's emotions. Obviously, the child expresses emotions through crying, smiling, laughing, and frowning. The parent, however, is constantly communicating to the child through her emotions, particularly through facial expressions. If a parent has a permanent scowl on her face, imagine the message this emotion is sending to the child!

There are three main functions of emotions. First is adaptation and survival. For example, fear is highly adaptive because of the clear link between feared events and possible threats to the child's well-being. It is argued that children express positive emotions and are visually pleasing to get their basic survival needs met. Second is regulation of information, in which children's emotions regulate the information they select from the perceptual world and the behaviors they display. For example, a child with an easy temperament will typically express positive emotions and elicit the same from others. On the other hand, a child with a difficult temperament will tend to illicit negative attention. The third function of emotions is communication. It is the primary way preverbal children express their feelings and needs.

A lack of responsiveness and reciprocity by the caregivers to the functions of emotions can result in the disturbance of their development. There are several adverse outcomes to delayed emotional development that relate to depression. The child may be unable to read the emotions of others or to express emotions in social situations. This leads to negative feedback from others, making the child feel like an outcast and not part of society. Children may express inappropriate emotions for situations and appear socially awkward and unsuccessful. Also, children have less ability to regulate the information they receive from the environment. One example of this is being unable to filter information that is unrelated to them or to personalize others' actions.

John Bowlby is an eminent researcher in the area of attachment and believes that insecure attachment and lack of love and affection in child rearing produce negative cognitive schemas that lead to depression. The combination of insecure attachment and the lack of emotional reciprocation results in negative psychological representations and expectations of negative outcomes. On the other hand, development of a secure attachment has been credited for the ability to regulate one's emotions. This is described in the following example.

Loss of attachment does not occur solely through poor parenting. The primary caregiver can go away for a number of reasons, such as death. A seven-year-old boy I worked with was referred for extreme lack of behavioral control in school. He would run out of his classroom, hide under desks, and lash out toward peers. At times he was quite dominant in his personality, while at other times he was quite passive. This happened every day. When I first met him he was playing in the principal's office. It did not take long for him to start his running and oppositional behavior pattern. In fact, at one point he got out of the building and was hiding on the playground, resulting in an all-out search for him. During the assessment it was discovered that the boy's parents were killed in a car accident when he was five years old; he had been riding in the back seat. He had seen the blood and his dead parents for some time while the accident was cleared. Indeed, this was a traumatic event, but what was most devastating for the child was the loss of the attachment with his mother. He exhibited many of the classic symptoms of attachment loss, including hoarding. Hoarding is when children collect items they feel are pertinent to their safety, as if preparing for a future "loss" disaster. He met the diagnostic criteria for agitated depression. It is important to note that loss during this period in development resulted in a significant lack of control of his emotions and behavior.

Depressotypic Organizations

The work of Dante Cicchetti is tremendously important to our current understanding of the development of depression in children because of his integration of multiple causal factors. As a result, his ideas are somewhat complicated. Many of his ideas were developed by conducting research on children of mothers with depression. In this section I will summarize the key aspects of his theory in a way that is directly applicable to parenting.

First, a few definitions. *Depressotypic* means indicative of depression. Another word sometimes used to mean depressotypic is *depressogenic*, or the making of depression. Depressotypic organization means that there are many variables, which will be described later, that can be organized in such a way as to cause depression in a child. As an example, an organization of variables that may lead to a motor vehicle accident could be (1) a tendency to drive fast, (2) drinking alcohol while driving, and (3) living in a location with lots of curved roads. You can see that the organization of these variables occurring together increases the risk of a person having an accident. It is easy to use your imagination to add variables that may increase the likelihood of an accident, such as rainy weather, lack of sleep, and using a car phone. A pattern or organization of the following, and obviously very different, variables is theorized to result in childhood depression.

An important assumption articulated by Cicchetti and discussed in other places in this book is that depression is not a unidimensional disorder (for example, different symptom patterns such as agitated versus retarded depression) and is likely caused through a variety of developmental pathways. This theory, therefore, does not rely on one system to explain depression. The aim is to integrate what is known about cognitive, emotional, interpersonal, and biological components of depression into a single unified theory. In this model of depression, Cicchetti proposes a system of four early developmental tasks that contribute to depression later in life. These four tasks are related to the organization of a child's psychological and biological development. How the child resolves each of these tasks influences how that particular system is incorporated into the child's personality and, in fact, influences how successful she will be when confronted with the next task. One of these tasks has to do with attachment, a concept described in detail earlier. If a secure attachment was developed, then the child will receive all its benefits and will be better prepared to meet the next challenge of developing self-awareness. After discussing these tasks and how they relate to the formation of a depressotypic organization, I will briefly describe three other systems that Cicchetti believes contribute to the development of depression.

Homeostatic and Physiological Regulation

The title of this task is a mouthful, but the essence of what is meant by it is extremely important. Homeostasis is a balance or equilibrium within a system. An example of homeostasis is a household thermostat. The thermostat turns on the heat when the house gets cold and shuts off the heat when the house reaches the correct temperature. It does this within only a few degrees' change from the set temperature. Imagine if the temperature had to change ten or fifteen degrees before the heater came on.

Maintaining a physiological homeostasis for an infant includes not getting too cold or too hot or eating when hungry. Infants are dependent on the caregiver to maintain homeostasis, and they request help as needed through emotional displays such as crying, fidgeting, and facial expressions. If the parent successfully listens to the child's emotional language, the child's brain will develop in a way that allows it to self-regulate. If the child's basic homeostatic needs are not met, however, the child will experience distress and exhibit negative emotional expressions, and brain development will not proceed in the way that properly allows for emotional self-regulation. Poor ability to self-regulate emotions in childhood remains a problem into middle childhood and adolescence. Specifically, these individuals experience high levels of guilt and sensitivity to the problems of others, and become overly empathetic. Children who cannot control their emotions may not be able to motivate themselves when feeling down or may be unable to control anger impulses. For example, a depressed adolescent who is getting teased may become so out of control that she will lash out at anybody she sees for several hours.

Affect Differentiation

Affect is the expression of emotions. After the child has met his needs for physiological homeostasis, the child begins to look toward the external world for stimulation. Affective or emotional expressions become a primary form of communication. At this point, the caregiver must be sensitive to the different states of arousal of his child that are triggered by the environment, including unfamiliar people and situations. The parent teaches the child how to express the proper emotion in these novel situations by imitation and selective attention. For example, when an unfamiliar uncle comes to visit, the parent smiles at the uncle and the infant and points at the uncle. The child learns that when a new person that the parent approves of approaches, the proper affect is smiling and happiness. This process could be described as emotional socialization. It works in the negative direction as well. When a parent expresses ambivalent emotions across a wide variety of situations, the child does not learn to differentiate the appropriate affective response for each one.

Secure Attachment

This developmental task is very similar to the attachment information described above. There are three types of attachment: secure, insecure-avoidant, and insecure-resistant. Only secure attachments are adaptive in this model. Development of a secure attachment results in the child being able to control his level of arousal and maintaining a feeling of security. For example, if you feel safe and secure, you do not need to maintain a high level of arousal. If you are out in Central Park after dark, however, and do not feel all that safe, you become aroused and you are very vigilant of your surroundings. Those who do not develop a secure attachment feel this way much of the time.

The type of attachment a child develops has far-reaching developmental implications. The child's experience of attachment becomes internalized and represented as an object. An internalized object is a profile or schema of how you expect people to act toward you. It is easy to imagine that children with insecure-resistant attachments do not expect people to meet their needs, and they actively resist developing emotional ties with people. Another example of this idea of internal representations has to do with how children view authority figures. It is common for children to view authority figures as threatening and scary, while it is even more common to see authority figures as supportive and helpful. You can think of these different views of authority figures as internalized objects or representations of those people. People develop a wide range of internalized objects, including parents, grandparents, men, women, peers, and siblings, among others. These internalized objects result in expectations about how interpersonal relationships are perceived and negotiated. This further leads to the thoughts and feelings associated with the outcome of an interpersonal meeting. To continue the authority figure example, if a depressed child with a hostile representation of authority figures is referred to the principal's office, one can expect the child to anticipate a harsh and demeaning encounter. Secure attachments, on the other hand, free individuals to develop consistent internalized objects and to safely experience interpersonal relationships without much prejudice from negative internalized objects.

Self-Awareness

During the second half of the second year of life, children begin to experience a differentiation between themselves and others. They develop internal objects or representations of themselves and of relationships between themselves and others. Also at this time, children are acquiring language and learning symbolic ways of expressing emotions. Language provides us with symbols, or words, for different abstract experiences, including emotions. There is substantial evidence that self-critical cognitive styles of parents are transmitted to their children. This results in internal representations of the self that are negative and constantly challenge one's self-esteem. Unfortunately, at this point in development the self-perceptions a child develops are enduring and resistant to change. It is incumbent on the caregiver to model realistic self-evaluation in both verbal and nonverbal ways. For example, you can say that you are satisfied with yourself, but then act argumentatively and disrespectfully toward your children. Despite the verbal message, the truth is clear to even a two-year-old.

At this point we have discussed the four important developmental tasks that must be overcome to prevent the promotion of depression. It should be clear that parenting styles are highly implicated in the onset of depression in this model. Cicchetti describes three other systems that must be considered in the development of depression: the microsystem, the exosystem, and the macrosystem. Don't let these terms scare you off—they are very straightforward and are important in understanding why children and adolescents become depressed.

The Microsystem

This term refers to the system of the child's immediate and extended family. A family history of depressive disorder is a significant indicator that one of the children will become depressed. In addition, there are several family variables that are predictive of depression. If a caregiver is suffering from some form of psychopathology, there is an increased risk that the child will be depressed. Research has shown that parental depression, anxiety, substance abuse, and criminal behavior are correlated with depression in children.

Other family factors include low socioeconomic status. Socioeconomic status is a family's economic standing compared to other families on variables such as family income, type of job (blue collar versus white collar), and level of parents' education. It is not the fact that these families have less money per se that predisposes a child to depression; rather, it is the increased stress put on the family system associated with meeting basic needs.

Families that are constantly in crisis or that experience negative life events are at greater risk of raising depressed children. Crisis-based families are those that have a very hard time solving their own problems. These families frequently seek social and financial support from state agency workers without trying to solve their problems first. This lack of problem solving may be due to a legitimate diminished capacity or may well be a conscious choice. A clear sign of a crisis-based family is when the parents visit several state-funded agencies in a single day and do this for weeks on end, so that it becomes an enduring lifestyle. Everything is a crisis. It is extremely stressful to the child to always be around people in this constant state of arousal.

The Exosystem

Cicchetti describes the exosystem as the child's ecology; that is, the environment outside of the family with which the child interacts. For children, this is primarily school. Thus, school environments are implicated in the onset of depression. Increases in rates of depression are seen when a child transitions from elementary school to middle school. Although some of this increase is accounted for by developmental and biological issues, the lack of a nurturing school environment can exacerbate or trigger a depressive episode. Research has shown that children who feel a certain connection with their school community tend to be better adjusted and experience less psychopathology.

Included in the exosystem is the availability of supportive services. Schools could increase the services available to children by taking advantage of what are known as "wraparound" services. There are a number of state- or city-funded and privately funded services available to children, but many families have a difficult time accessing these services. By providing some space in the school to house these services, children could have access to them more readily, and this would foster a greater connection with the school. In fact, in situations where wraparound services are implemented, many families historically disenfranchised from the school come to the school more frequently and feel more free to take part in their children's education.

In rural settings there may not be the availability of services found in larger cities. This constitutes an exosystem that may protect children less from depression. Of course, one could argue that there may be less stressors and more favorable student-teacher ratios in a rural environment, leading to less need for services.

The Macrosystem

The macrosystem includes the values and norms held by a culture. Although there is little research support for the influence of cultural variables on the manifestation of depression, this idea is intuitively appealing. Specifically, the political climate may result in differences in the availability of resources for education about and prevention of mental illness. Further, economic changes may put increased stressors on already stressed families. It would be hard to dispute that the Great Depression did not result in emotional as well as economic depression.

Research on suicide has shown that suicide increases in situations where the traditional culture has deteriorated and been replaced by a more industrialized and urban one. For example, suicides are higher in the Northeast than they are in the more rural South. Cicchetti says this suggests that the absence of traditional supports may result in increased risk of poor adjustment and depression.

Summary of the Developmental Models of Depression

From the perspective of child development, there are several important tasks a child must master to protect himself from depression. These tasks cannot be mastered without the significant help and attention of the parent. The following summarizes these tasks and what a parent should do to encourage her child's mastery of them.

- Meet the child's basic physiological needs such as eating and comfort without the child having to express a lot of negative emotions. This requires the parent to be attuned to the child's emotional ways of communicating and to meet the child's needs relatively promptly. This allows the child to develop the ability to self-regulate his emotions. The early effort to meet the child's needs may save a tremendous amount of effort that will be expended if the child does not develop this ability.

- Socialize the child to express and respond to a wide range of affective displays. The parent does this by showing the child how to express a variety of emotions appropriate to the situation and to mimic the child's emotional displays when they are appropriate.

- Develop a secure attachment between the child and the caregiver. Here the parent must be consistent and responsive to the child. This may require the caregiver to overcome differences between the child's temperament and the parent's temperament. Also, major losses and a lack of comfort contact can result in insecure attachments.

- Develop appropriate self-awareness in the child and help her differentiate self from others. Parents do this by teaching the child a range of symbols (words) to represent emotions and to appropriately model a positive sense of self through their words, expressions, and actions. A parent with reasonable self-esteem will teach a child to have reasonable self-esteem.

These tasks are related to the organization of the child's psychological and biological systems. Three other systems have an impact on the development of depression, and they are summarized below.

- The microsystem is the immediate and extended family. A family history of depression is a significant risk factor for childhood depression. Also, families where members experience psychopathology, families in frequent crisis, and families of low socioeconomic status are at risk of raising children with depression.

- The exosystem is the child's immediate community, including school and social supports. It is important that a child feel connected to his school community to prevent depression. Further, the availability of support systems can reduce the stress of school and result in lowered probability of depression.
- The macrosystem has to do with the culture in which the child is raised. It has been shown that cultures that have shed their traditional heritage put people at risk of suicide and, presumably, depression.

The developmental theory of depression is very comprehensive and useful in understanding what makes children depressed. Despite the breadth of this theory, it does not explain everything. I believe that it explains, along with the biological model to be discussed next, the genesis of the diathesis toward depression; that is, the psychological and biological vulnerability that is triggered by stress and results in depression. Other theories of depression explain more about how the child experiences depression cognitively and behaviorally and suggest more reactive treatments than recommended by the developmental model described above.

BIOLOGICAL MODELS OF DEPRESSION

There is little question that there is a biological aspect to depression. As described in the previous section, there is an increased risk of depression when an immediate or extended family member has it. There are three primary issues to consider when thinking about the biology of depression. The first is genetics. Is there a particular gene or set of genes that predisposes a person to depression? The second has to do with neurotransmitters. Does too much or too little of the chemicals that transmit information between brain cells account for depression? Third has to do with hormones. Are there specific chemicals that flow throughout the body that cause depression? These are the questions we will address in this section.

Genetics and Depression

Most scientists who study depression believe that it has a genetic component. Genes are the part of human DNA (the master code for a human) that synthesize proteins and result in every process and structure of the human body. Because there are so many forms of depression, it is not expected that only one gene will be found to account for all depression. Most likely there will be a variety of genes working together or operating at different times that will best explain different types of depression.

At this time, however, these genes have not been conclusively identified. There is some evidence that one or more of the genes on chromosomes 18 and 21 make a person vulnerable to bipolar disorder. It is important to discover the genes that account for depression for a number of reasons. First, the diagnosis of depression will be aided as our ability to analyze one's genes increases. Second, more precise information will be available for genetic counseling of parents. Third, the future may provide for genetic engineering to remove the possibility of depression. Although hotly debated, the chance of heading off depression before birth has some appeal.

Without having yet identified the genes, how are we so sure that there is a genetic component to depression? By studying family linkages, twins, and adopted children, researchers can show with little doubt that depression is passed down through families genetically.

As an example, twin studies compare the rates at which both of identical twins and fraternal twins have depression. Identical twins behave genetically as identical individuals because they are derived from a single fertilized egg; that is, they share the same genetic material. Fraternal twins come from two different eggs and only share half of the same genetic material. Thus, they are no different than siblings genetically. Studies of this kind have been typically conducted on twins with bipolar disorder. When rates of bipolar disorder are compared between identical twins and fraternal twins, there is an amazing result. Identical twins both experience bipolar disorder between 50 and 92.5 percent of the time. On the other hand, fraternal twins both experience bipolar disorder between 0 and 38.5 percent of the time. This finding is true both for twins that are reared in the same home or those reared apart. This is strong evidence that genes play a part in depression.

Neurotransmitters and Depression

Neurotransmitters are the chemicals that are instrumental in communication between brain cells called neurons. The human brain has billions of neurons. They secrete neurotransmitters at one end, and the receiving neuron temporarily binds with the neurotransmitter to receive the message. What is hard to imagine about neurotransmitters is that each single molecule has the responsibility to bind like a key in a lock with the receiving neuron and send the message along. (I hesitate to use the term *chemical* when referring to neurotransmitters because it can be misconstrued that the brain is using large quantities of these neurotransmitters like vinegar and oil are used in salad dressing. In this example, one has to have the right amount of vinegar and the right amount of oil for the dressing to taste good. It does not work this way in the human brain. Neurotransmitters are only present in certain parts of the brain, and the balance of one neurotransmitter to another has nothing to do with the cause of depression. Unlike vinegar and oil, the problems with neurotransmitters lie in how they are metabolized or how much of them are produced in a particular part of the brain. Thus, the overused term *chemical imbalance* really does not make sense.)

There are two neurotransmitters implicated in depression, norepinephrine and serotonin. The problem arises when there are not enough of these neurotransmitters in the gap between two communicating neurons (called the synaptic cleft) to send the message. The simple answer, then, is to increase the amount of these neurotransmitters in the synaptic cleft. This is what antidepressants do through a variety of mechanisms.

The first inkling that neurotransmitters were involved in depression was in the 1950s. It was discovered that when a patient took a drug called reserpine he became very depressed. Reserpine reduced the class of neurotransmitters called monoamines. You should note that norepinephrine and serotonin are two of the neurotransmitters in the monoamine class. Based on this information, the first antidepressants were developed, called monoamine oxidase inhibitors (MAOIs). Since the neurobiological problem that causes depression is not enough neurotransmitters, the first antidepressants prevented the mechanism in the brain cell that destroys monoamines. By doing this there was an increase in the available monoamines for sending messages between cells. Monoamine oxidase inhibitors are still used today, but they are typically the drug of last resort. This is because they are not very "clean," which means they affect many brain systems in addition to the ones associated with depression (these unintended effects are commonly known as side effects). The goal then became to better understand the specifics of which monoamines caused depression.

The relationship between norepinephrine and depression has been supported by the development of drugs that selectively block the removal of norepinephrine from the synaptic cleft. Keeping the neurotransmitter in the synaptic cleft longer is another way to increase the needed neurotransmitter to facilitate communication between two neurons. This is, in fact, how most of the newest antidepressants work.

The neurotransmitter serotonin has been implicated in depression in the same way as norepinephrine. Serotonin-specific reuptake inhibitors (SSRI) drugs result in substantial reductions in depressive symptoms, with the added benefit of few side effects. Antidepressant drugs that work in this way include Prozac, Zoloft, Serzone, Paxil, and Luvox. It is believed that increases in serotonin levels directly relieve depression as well as increase the availability of norepinephrine by influencing connected pathways in the brain. The newest antidepressants available, such as Effexor, target both serotonin and norepinephrine. The advantages and disadvantages of antidepressant treatment will be discussed in the chapter on treatment of depression. It is clear, however, that the identification of the neurotransmitters implicated in depression has opened up an important treatment option.

Hormones and Depression

The body's response to threats is activated by hormones. The classic response to a threat is "fight or flight"; that is, your body becomes ready either to stand ground and directly confront a threat or to run away from the threat. The specific brain system that responds to stress and results in the secretion of hormones is called the hypothalamic-pituitary-adrenal (HPA) axis. The HPA axis lies at the base of your brain just above your mouth and includes the part of the brain called the hypothalamus and two glands that are connected to the brain called the pituitary and adrenal glands. The hormonal response to stress is rather complicated, but suffice it to say that when the brain perceives a threat, the HPA axis starts pumping out hormones.

Interestingly, researchers have found that the hormones released by the HPA axis are chronically elevated in depressed individuals. The specific chemical that researchers believe is related to depression is the corticotropin-releasing factor (CRF) secreted by the hypothalamus. Evidence shows that in response to antidepressant medication, CRF levels decrease in depressed individuals. Further, CRF causes some of the primary symptoms of depression, including insomnia, decreased appetite, and anxiety.

No treatments have been derived from the information about CRF, but the findings lend considerable support to the biological underpinnings of depression as well as to the diathesis-stress model described in chapter 1. Since depressed individuals are chronically producing too much CRF, when they are put under stress the production of CRF is further increased. Important research by Charles Nemeroff of Emory University has indicated that stressors in individuals with already increased CRF production can permanently further increase CRF production. Thus, these individuals are predisposed to become depressed (diathesis), and a stressor can increase the body's production of CRF and incite the depressive episode. Because the change in CRF production is relatively permanent, depression becomes a chronic cycle.

BEHAVIORAL THEORIES OF DEPRESSION

Although you would be right to assume that all psychologists study behavior, behavioral theories of depression focus on the role of learning in the understanding of human endeavors. Unlike other theorists who assume there are unseen motives, needs, and drives that influence behavior, behavioral psychologists focus on overt behavior as the unit of study. These theorists assert that it is not necessary to posit covert processes, such as drives and motives, to understand and modify behavior. Although there has been a tremendous amount of research completed by behavioral psychologists, there are primarily three different behavioral psychology explanations of childhood depression. These are classical conditioning, operant conditioning, and social learning theory.

Classical Conditioning

Classical conditioning is the original type of behavioral psychology. At the turn of the twentieth century, a Russian physiologist, Ivan Pavlov, conducted studies on the digestive processes of dogs. In his laboratory, Pavlov harnessed the dogs and inserted tubes into their jaws to catch saliva. He then gave the dogs meat powder and began to measure their saliva. Day after day, Pavlov and his assistants came into the room to give their dogs food and to measure the amount of saliva the dogs secreted. Pavlov soon realized that his dogs began to salivate when he walked into the room, before they were given any meat powder to salivate over. Pavlov serendipitously realized that the dogs had associated the sound of the door opening with the meat being served to them. Now the dogs salivated over the door being opened. Thus, the dogs learned and reacted on a physiological level. Pavlov coined the term *conditioning* and the type of learning he discovered is referred to as classical conditioning. In this type of learning, the organism (dog or human) learns about the environment by passively sitting back and responding to what the setting offers. Pavlov and other researchers continued to explore classical conditioning, developing experiments that they believed were analogous to humans. One particular study has been cited as an explanation of depression from the perspective of classical conditioning. In this study, the experimenter taught the dog that meat would be provided when a circle was presented. The dog would be shocked electrically, however, when an oval was presented. Once trained to expect these contingencies, the experimenter then gradually changed the shape of the objects, making the circle more and more oval and the oval more and more circular, until they were nearly impossible for the dogs to differentiate. Pavlov noticed that as the circles and ovals approached the same shape and the dog could not anticipate whether he would receive meat or a shock, the dogs demonstrated restlessness and agitation, and bit at themselves. Pavlov asserted that psychological distress, including depression, was the result of being unable to predict and manage the contingencies the real world offers us. From the perspective of classical conditioning, a child may demonstrate depression as a result of ambiguity and inconsistency in the way rewards and punishments are offered. For example, if a child comes to believe a parent is loving and caring, but occasionally the parent is aggressive and mean without warning, the child may become upset and, if this occurs regularly, depressed. Therapists who work with children of alcoholics see this phenomenon. At five o'clock the child has a parent that is stressed from a hard day at work and wants to be left alone. At 6:30, the same parent, now nursing his second or third drink, is warm and amusing the child by telling stories. By 8:00, the same parent, now into his sixth drink, is irritable and yelling for no apparent reason. The child, who has remained virtually the same throughout the evening, has seen the same parent push him away, pull him back in, then yell and threaten him. Often, these children are depressed and yearn for affection, but they fear approaching the parent.

Operant Conditioning

A more recent behavioral theory is that of B. F. Skinner, who recognized that people are not passive organisms, harnessed like Pavlov's dogs. Instead, they operate on their environments and, in doing so, learn what payoffs are available to them. His theory of behavior is referred to as operant conditioning or trial-and-error learning. He asserted that we tend to do things that feel good and tend to avoid doing things that bring us pain. In Skinner's world, people, including children, go about the business of exploring their world, finding out what feels good and doing it as much as they can. On the other hand, when we run into situations that bring us pain, we tend to avoid them in the future. According to Skinner and his adherents, depression occurs when we are unable to create or find situations that bring us pleasure. After repeatedly trying and failing, we tend to give up. Having given up, we are no longer trying, and when we don't try to bring pleasure into our lives, there is very little joy in them. In particular, these psychologists examined the importance of social contact. It is crucial that people receive recognition and affirmation from others. According to these researchers, depression occurs when the person cannot find a way to gain the acceptance and attention of those with whom they desire to interact. After trying again and again, only to fail, they give up. Having given up, they tend to get little or none of the acceptance they so desperately want. Imagine a teenage girl who moves into a new community. Like any other child, she wants the acceptance of the other girls in her class. If she tries to break into the group but is rejected, she may try once or twice more, but sooner or later she gives up. Not surprisingly, this youngster is a prime candidate for becoming depressed. From the perspective of operant conditioning, try as she might, she cannot find the key to receiving the reward, and she becomes depressed.

Social Learning Theory

A third way of understanding depression from a behavioral perspective is social learning theory, which is typically associated with Albert Bandura. For Bandura, behavior, including depression, can be understood by looking at the interaction between the person and the environment. He believed that just as the environment shapes the person, the person shapes the environment. Consider for a moment the numerous ways that your child's behavior shapes your behavior as a parent, and you can then appreciate Bandura's perspective. Another major contribution from Bandura was the concept of modeling, which is learning by watching others. Recall that Pavlov understood the type of learning involving passively having others reward and punish us, and Skinner articulated trial-and-error learning. Now imagine trying to understand learning to drive a car through either of these models. It would take us hours, perhaps days, just to find where to put the key and to turn it. Obviously, we learn much of our behaviors by observing others. Anyone who has children can appreciate the experience of being amazed (and sometimes embarrassed) at what our children learn from us and mimic (seemingly at just the wrong time). From the perspective of social learning theory, childhood depression may be the result of observing ineffective ways of coping with life's difficulties by others, including parents or friends. By the time children reach their teens, they have had thousands of opportunities to see how to deal with problems, and often these role models are coping in dysfunctional ways that lead to depression.

A number of approaches to the treatment of depression are derived from a behavioral model of depression. They include:

- *Daily monitoring*—keeping a journal or log of pleasant events that occur throughout the day.
- *Relaxation training*—using one of several techniques (deep breathing, aromatherapy, meditation, positive daydreaming, or massage therapy) to relax and reduce one's stress and anxiety.
- *Managing aversive events*—learning not to overreact to situations that cause upset.
- *Time management*—learning to organize your day so that you are more productive and less overwhelmed by necessary chores.

- *Increased pleasant activities*—scheduling time and planning for enjoyable pastimes.

COGNITIVE THEORY OF DEPRESSION

A powerful perspective on childhood depression is cognitive theory. According to cognitive theorists, much of our reality is constructed by our thoughts and how we think about things. Whether we see the cup as half empty or half full is, at its heart, a cognitive theorist's perspective. For them, how and what we think determine how we feel, which in turn, determines what we do. Here is a simple example. If I believe that I am lousy at math, when faced with a difficult math problem I am likely to put forth little effort because I have already assumed that it is too difficult and I will fail. If I put forth little effort, chances are I will tend to fail more often than another person with comparable math skills but a more positive outlook. Having put forth little effort and thereby failing, I reinforce the self-perception that I am lousy at math; my self-defeating attitude toward math continues. On the other hand, another person with comparable math skills but a more optimistic outlook puts forth more effort, gets some math questions correct, and gradually improves his math skills and his self-confidence. In this way, cognitive theorists say, we construct our own reality.

Several cognitive psychologists have examined specific cognitive processes that are directly relevant to childhood depression, including Albert Ellis, Aaron Beck, Donald Meichenbaum, and Martin Seligman. In the 1950s, Albert Ellis developed rational emotive therapy, an approach to treating depression and anxiety designed to rid an individual of these disorders by ridding the person of irrational and self-defeating ideas. Ellis emphasized the role of cognition on behavior. In contrast to his behavioral psychology colleagues who understood human actions in terms of behaviors, rewards, and punishments, Ellis introduced the idea that human behavior is largely the result of how we interpret events. For Ellis, an event occurred and was then interpreted by the observer. The event is processed through the mind of the observer. Of course, each person's interpretation of the event is biased, based on one's immediate state of mind and history. From this interpretation, the person responds. It is not the event to which we respond, it is our interpretation of it.

Ellis asserted that there is a clear and direct relationship between our thoughts, feelings, and behavior. If we think depressing thoughts, we will become depressed and will behave like a depressed person. In turn, he believed that if you modify one of these three major functions of living (thinking, feeling, or behaving), it is inevitable that the other two functions will change. For Ellis and other cognitive psychologists, thinking was the point of attack. Ellis believed that people are naturally predisposed to thinking about themselves and the world in healthy and rational ways, but that social institutions such as the family, schools, and the media bombard the child with irrational and self-defeating notions.

From Ellis's perspective, there are three primary disturbance-producing irrational ideas: demandingness, awfulizing, and self-rating. Demandingness is the tendency to believe that we must or should have what we actually only want to have. It is the erroneous tendency to think that we cannot live without what we really only want. The person is illogically saying, "Because I want something, I cannot live without it." This type of thinking creates false urgency and despair when wishes are not fulfilled. "Awfulizing" is the tendency to think that things must be a certain way and when things aren't the way they should be it is awful. When the awfulizing person sees something as awful, there is a further tendency to make the awful thing the center of focus, and, from this, the whole world is seen as awful. Now, rather than one specific thing not meeting expectations, the person thinks, "My whole life is awful." A final aspect of awfulizing is the belief that if expectations are not met and things are awful, life becomes intolerable and unbearable. A third type of irrational thinking is self-rating, the near-universal and illogical act of rating one's self as either good or bad for doing or not doing what "should" have been done. Clinicians target self-rating not to discourage evaluating one's own performance, rather, to confront the tendency to overgeneralize and categorize oneself as either good or bad, based on a specific action. At best, the evaluation should be limited to the domain in question: "I have difficulty with my multiplication tables," instead of "I am stupid." The goal of rational emotive therapy is to assist and guide the individual in searching out her own irrational beliefs and replacing them with rational self-statements that lead to healthier living.

Soon after Ellis, Aaron Beck elaborated on the role of cognition in causing depression. For Beck, depression is the result of viewing the self, the future, and the world in an unrealistically negative manner. This view was referred to by Beck as the negative triad (themselves, the world, the future). Depressed people see themselves as unworthy, incapable, and undesirable. They see the world in equally negative terms, and they don't expect that it will get any better. Beck described the following common errors in the way depressed people process information; that is, flaws in the logic of depressed people.

- *Arbitrary infererence*—drawing a conclusion in the absence of evidence or when evidence is contrary to the conclusion.
- *Selective abstraction*—the tendency to focus on a negative detail in a situation and to conceptualize the entire experience on the basis of this negative fragment.
- *Overgeneralization*—the tendency to draw a general rule or conclusion on the basis of one isolated incident and to apply the concept indiscriminately to both related and unrelated situations.
- *Magnification and minimization*—the tendency to overestimate the significance of undesirable events and to underestimate the significance of desirable events.
- *Personalization*—the tendency to relate external events to oneself without evidence.
- *All-or-nothing thinking*—the tendency to see things in absolute, black-or-white, all-or-nothing terms.

These logical errors are believed to be the cause of the depression-prone person's tendency to interpret events in extreme, negative, categorical, and judgmental ways.

Donald Meichenbaum is credited with developing cognitive behavior modification, a blend of cognitive and behavioral approaches to understanding and treating depression. Cognitive behavior modification uses behavioral techniques to modify depressogenic (depression-causing) thinking. Like his cognitive counterparts,

Meichenbaum believes that depression is caused primarily by negative "self-talk," misinterpretation of events, and distorted or irrational thinking. He uses behavioral approaches to modify the thinking of the depressed individual. Some of the specific approaches used in cognitive behavior modification include:

- *Relabeling or reframing*—generating alternative and more positive interpretations of events.
- *Anticatastrophic reappraisal*—teaching the person to resist the urge to quickly jump to an extreme, negative, and unlikely conclusion.
- *Thought-stopping*—recognizing and interrupting negative self-statements, overlaying them with more honest and positive self-statements.

A recent contributor to the cognitive understanding of depression is Martin Seligman. Early in his career, Seligman gained notoriety for his concept of learned helplessness. More recently, he developed an extension of his thinking which is referred to as learned optimism. According to Seligman, depression is the result of specific ways that the individual reacts to setbacks. His theory focuses on what the individual attributes the setback to—that is, what the person sees as the cause of his failure. This determines whether the person will become depressed. Drawing on the work of others, Seligman gives attention to three explanatory dimensions. First, the cause may be something about the person (internal explanation), or it may be something about the situation or circumstances (external explanation). Second, the cause may be a factor that will persist over time (stable explanation), or it may be a transient event (unstable explanation). Finally, the cause may affect a number of outcomes (global explanation), or it may be restricted to the event being interpreted (specific explanation). How the person interprets good and bad events affects the individual. If a child generates an internal explanation for a bad occurrence ("I failed the test because I am stupid"), the child increases the risk of damaging his self-esteem. If the child uses an external explanation for the same occurrence ("I failed the test because my teacher writes bad tests"), the child's self-esteem may remain intact. Stable explanations ("I failed the test because I have always been stupid") lead to more chronic and unalterable attributions than do unstable explanations ("I failed the test because I didn't study"). Global explanations ("I failed the test because I can't do anything") lead to a more pervasive sense of incompetence than specific explanations ("I have difficulty with long division"). In his early work, *Learned Helplessness,* Seligman offered an understanding of how an internal, stable, and global attribution style leads to depression. His more recent work, *Learned Optimism,* offers help through specific approaches designed to turn pessimists into optimists through confronting negative thinking.

CHAPTER 4

EMOTIONAL PROBLEMS THAT MAY OCCUR WITH DEPRESSION

Unfortunately, in children, emotional problems tend to occur in packs. Overall, 40 to 70 percent of children and adolescents with depression experience some other diagnosable emotional problem. Between 20 to 50 percent experience two or more psychiatric disorders in addition to their depression. Comorbidity is the term used to describe the occurrence of more than one disorder at the same time for an individual. The term *comorbidity* will be used in this chapter to describe disorders that co-occur with depression in children. The descriptions of these emotional problems are adapted from the *Diagnostic and Statistical Manual of Mental Disorders, Fourth Edition (DSM-IV)*.

The most frequently occurring class of emotional problems comorbid with depression are anxiety disorders. Of the anxiety disorders, the most frequent comorbid problem is separation anxiety. The second most frequently observed class of disorders comorbid with depression are the disruptive disorders. Of the disruptive disorders, the most common is conduct disorder. Another frequent comorbid disorder for adolescents is substance abuse. Without trying to complicate the issue, it is important to point out that when dysthymic disorder occurs with major depression, it is technically considered a comorbid condition. This is because there are separate criteria for each of the disorders. (Comorbidity of dysthymic disorder and major depression was discussed in chapter 2 under the heading Double Depression.)

One way to understand why so many children experience more than one emotional disorder has to do with their personality development. Children are developing in many ways including brain development, physical development, and personality development. As we discussed in chapter 3 regarding the developmental theories of depression, early events go a long way to determine if a child will be depressed. A child's personality, however, has not completely formed until much later in the developmental period, such as late adolescence or early adulthood. Therefore, neither comorbid disorder comprises the full expression of the diathesis. Although many of the internalizing disorders as well as some of the externalizing disorders share a similar biological substrate, it is, in part, the continued experience of stressors throughout the developmental period that defines what will be the prominent emotional problem in later years.

THE IMPACT OF COMORBIDITY

In addition to complicating treatment, comorbidity is indicative of several unfavorable clinical outcomes. Children with comorbid problems are at a greater risk for relapse of a major depressive episode. In addition, these children tend to have longer depressive episodes. Where a typical depressive episode for a child may last between nine and twelve months, in cases of comorbidity the cycle of episodes may last as long as two years. Children and adolescents with comorbid disorders such as anxiety and conduct disorder are at a greater risk for substance abuse, suicide, and poor social skills development than children with just depression.

ANXIETY DISORDERS

Anxiety disorders include separation anxiety disorder, panic disorder, phobias, obsessive-compulsive disorder, and generalized anxiety disorders (GAD), and all may be comorbid with depression. The most common comorbid anxiety disorder seen in children is separation anxiety disorder, found in approximately 36 percent of children with depression. Negative affectivity, described in chapter 2, is a specific type of mixed depressive and anxiety disorder that is diagnosed using primarily personality testing and parenting history information; it is considered a separate form of depression and thus is not included in the anxiety disorders. The comorbid anxiety disorders in this chapter can be diagnosed by themselves. This is a subtle but important distinction for those who conduct research on depression.

Those with an anxiety disorder exhibit motor, physiological, and cognitive symptoms. As with depression, each type of anxiety disorder displays more or less of each type of symptom. The following summarizes the symptoms of anxiety.

- *Motor symptoms:* trembling, nail biting, thumb sucking, stuttering, clenched jaw, and avoidance of others.

- *Physiological symptoms:* increased heart rate, sweating, change in muscle tension, increased respiration, breathless- ness, nausea, vomiting, stomachache, and frequent urination.
- *Cognitive symptoms:* thoughts of being scared, expecting danger, feeling inadequate or incompetent, and images of bodily injury.

Research has shown that children with both depression and anx- iety experience even more physical complaints (somatic complaints) than would be expected from just depressed children the same age. Specifically, the most frequent symptoms are lightheadedness or dizziness, upset stomach, and back pain. Other common symptoms include stomach pains, vomiting, and menstrual problems. Research has shown that the more severe the anxiety and depression, the more severe the symptoms. This has important implications for identifying children with emotional problems. Children who are frequently home sick from school with these diffuse physical com- plaints or who frequently visit the school nurse for similar prob- lems should be evaluated for depression and anxiety. A child with previously diagnosed depression exhibiting even more than the expected physical complaints should be evaluated for comorbid anxiety as well. In both cases, the treatment may change as a result of the diagnosis.

It is important to recognize that children and adolescents nor- mally experience a wide variety of fears and anxieties. Research has shown that children experience on average as many as ten different fears and excessive worries at a time. Also, the nature of these worries changes over the developmental period. Interestingly, anxiety is also appropriate, to an extent, for success on cognitive or physical activities; that is, some anxiety actually enhances one's performance on cognitive or physical tasks. Some anxiety is normal and expected. However, too much anxiety is detrimental to performance. A parent should not overreact to anxiety, but when it is significant and impairs some aspect of the child's functioning, it should be considered a problem.

Through the developmental period, the onset of anxiety in children with comorbid anxiety and depression tends to occur prior to the onset of depression. Issues related to security of attachment and the strong physiological aspects (motor and somatic symptoms) of anxiety facilitate the expression of anxiety symptoms earlier than depression for infants or toddlers.

Separation Anxiety Disorder

Separation anxiety is diagnosed when a child experiences more than developmentally expected anxiety when separated from the person with whom he or she is attached. Typical symptoms seen in separation anxiety include:

- excessive distress when parents leave or are expected to leave
- worry about harm or death toward attachment figures
- worry about being kidnapped or getting lost
- reluctance or refusal to go to school
- fear of being home without the parents
- reluctance or refusal to go to sleep without the parent nearby
- nightmares about separation from parent
- frequent physical complaints when away from parents

The key factor here is determining what is normal anxiety for the developmental phase. Particularly during the first two years (during the critical development of a secure attachment), there should be little diagnostic concern about expressions of distress by the child. The child's needs must be met during this period, and if the child is expressing distress, it is not because of a separation anxiety; rather, it is because the child's needs are not met.

Panic Disorder

Panic disorder is a form of anxiety with prominent motor and physiological symptoms known as a panic attack that can last from minutes to hours. Panic is different from other types of anxiety in that the onset of symptoms is sudden. Thus, a child will experience a host of these symptoms all at once and seemingly from out of nowhere. A child must experience more than one panic attack to be diagnosed. Panic attacks are characterized by a number of symptoms, including:

- accelerated heart rate
- sweating
- trembling or shaking
- sensations of shortness of breath or smothering
- feeling of choking
- chest pain or discomfort
- nausea or abdominal distress
- feeling dizzy, unsteady, lightheaded, or faint
- derealization (feelings of unreality) or depersonalization (being detached from oneself)

- fear of losing control or going crazy
- fear of dying
- numbness or tingling sensations
- chills or hot flashes

Furthermore, following panic attacks, these children are troubled by:

- persistent concern about having additional attacks
- worry about the implications of the attack or its consequences (losing control, having a heart attack, "going crazy")
- significant change in behavior related to the attacks

Panic disorders are very treatable with behavioral psychotherapy and medication. A prominent result of panic is that some children begin to avoid situations that are associated with the panic attacks, including school and other public places. In severe cases, the child may be extremely reluctant to leave home.

Phobias

Phobias include fears of specific things or situations, such as fears of snakes or heights. They also include fears of social contact and represent a frequent comorbid symptom of depression, particularly in those children with poor social skills and extreme feelings of worthlessness.

Social phobia is characterized by a significant and persistent fear of one or more social or performance situations in which the child is exposed to unfamiliar people or to possible scrutiny by others.

The child fears that he or she will act in a way that will be humiliating or embarrassing. For children with social phobia, exposure to the feared social situation almost invariably provokes anxiety, which may take the form of a situationally bound panic attack. Unlike adults with social phobia, who recognize that their fear is excessive or unreasonable, children may see their fear as quite reasonable. Out of their fear, children avoid these situations or endure them with intense distress. Understandably, the avoidance, anxious anticipation, or distress in the feared situations interferes significantly with the person's performance.

Obsessive-Compulsive Disorder

Children who experience obsessive-compulsive disorder (OCD) may suffer from obsessions, compulsions, or both. Obsessions are recurrent and persistent thoughts, impulses, or images that are intrusive and cause marked anxiety or distress. The thoughts, impulses, or images are not simply excessive worries about real-life problems. In fact, oftentimes these thoughts are irrational and contrary to reality. For example, one child's thoughts centered around the worry that she would accidentally mail her brother away in an envelope. To cope with these bothersome thoughts, the child attempts to ignore or suppress them or to neutralize them with some other thought or action.

Compulsions are repetitive behaviors such as hand washing, ordering or organizing things, and repeated checking or mental acts such as praying, counting, or repeating words silently. The compulsive child feels driven to perform in response to an obsession, at times in accordance with rules that are rigidly applied. Often, the compulsive behaviors are aimed at preventing or reducing distress or avoiding some dreaded event or situation. Typically, a child with obsessive-compulsive disorder recognizes that these thoughts and behaviors are excessive and unreasonable. Further, he experiences marked distress as the thoughts and behaviors are time consuming, easily taking more than an hour a day, and significantly interfere with the child's normal routine, academic functioning, and social activities.

Children with depression and obsessive-compulsive disorder have been known to repeat or dwell on self-depreciating thoughts as well as to not be able to let go of an embarrassing situation. For example, if a child with OCD is embarrassed in class, the embarrassment may plague the child's thoughts for several hours or days. When you talk to a child suffering from this problem and try to determine why there has been a change in behavior, you may be surprised to find she is still dwelling on the embarrassing situation that occurred several days prior.

Another obsessive-compulsive pattern seen in children with comorbid depression and OCD has been called *folie du doute* or doubting mania. Children with doubting mania will repeatedly check to see if doors are closed, if they have their homework in their backpacks, if they are late for school, or if they made a mistake. That is, they doubt that they have done correctly what they indeed have done. This is an easily seen overt sign of obsessive-compulsive disorder.

Generalized Anxiety Disorder (GAD)

Generalized anxiety disorder is the clinical term associated with general or nonspecific anxiety. Unlike children with specific phobias, children with generalized anxiety disorder worry about a wide range of events or activities, such as school performance, physical appearence, and social interactions. Children with GAD are often overly tense or uptight. Some may seek a lot of reassurance, and their worries may interfere with activities. Adolescents often know that their worries are unrealistic and inappropriate. The important feature to making this diagnosis is knowing what is normal anxiety for a child's particular developmental phase. In addition to having difficulty controlling worry, children with generalized anxiety disorder may experience:

- restlessness or feeling keyed up or on edge
- being easily fatigued
- difficulty concentrating or mind going blank
- irritability
- muscle tension
- frequent physical complaints
- sleep disturbance (difficulty falling or staying asleep, or restless, unsatisfying sleep)

DISRUPTIVE DISORDERS

Disruptive disorders are the second most frequent psychiatric condition comorbid with depression. Disruptive disorders have been described as externalizing disorders because the behavior problem is expressed outwardly; hence the term "acting out" is also applied to the behavior of children diagnosed with disruptive disorders. Estimates of the frequency of comorbidity with depression range from 10 to 80 percent. This is an extremely wide range and exemplifies the difficulties in differentiating depression from disruptive disorders, as well as the potential similarities in biological causes. It is easy to see, given what we have discussed about depression so far, why a child would be disruptive. Depressed children are frequently irritable, they often do not feel there is any point to their lives, they often have poor ability to modulate their emotional reactions, and they typically lack coping skills.

Irritability can lead to simple refusal and disrespect indicative of oppositional-defiant disorder to extremely violent acts toward others due to frustration. In the latter case, the behavior is more indicative of conduct disorder. Children and adolescents who feel hopeless and that their lives are meaningless frequently do not consider the consequences of their behavior toward themselves (risk taking) or toward others (violating the rights of others). The inability to modulate one's emotions can result in impulsive acts, seen in attention-deficit/hyperactivity disorder, and can result in violent acts toward others, as seen in conduct disorder. Finally, the inability to cope leads to feelings of helplessness and frustration. At these times, delinquent and aggressive acts are the last resort for some depressed children or adolescents.

Another important issue related to disruptive disorders and depression has to do with which came first. As described above, one can imagine why a depressed child becomes oppositional or aggressive. This is not the only way, however, in which a child or adolescent who exhibits depression gets diagnosed with oppositional-defiant disorder or conduct disorder. The other case is when a conduct-disordered or antisocial child gets depressed. Depression in a child who is first a criminal or antisocial is very common. There are typically only a few symptoms of depression, and the depression is most frequently expressed when the child is caught and thus not allowed to act in a criminal way. At other times, children with disruptive behavior will not receive much reinforcement from their environments and may experience symptoms of depression.

The best example of this phenomenon is incarcerated youth. In almost every case they will show some signs of depression due to their incarceration. This does not mean their crimes are related to depression or that they should be excused. In many cases, the depression is only a secondary symptom of being conduct-disordered or antisocial. How this works is very complicated and a topic for a whole other book. The basic mechanisms of this problem have to do with similarities between biological and developmental causes of depression and aggression as well as the underlying depression that is frequently seen in disorders of personality, including antisocial personality disorder.

Oppositional-Defiant Disorder

Children with oppositional-defiant disorder (ODD) display a pattern of negativistic, hostile, and defiant behavior. Symptoms of oppositional-defiant disorder include:

- loses temper
- often argues with adults
- often actively defies or refuses to comply with adults' requests or rules
- often deliberately annoys people
- often blames others for his mistakes or misbehavior

- is often touchy or easily annoyed by others
- is often angry and resentful
- is often spiteful or vindictive

Oppositional-defiant disorder tends to appear developmentally prior to its more virulent partner, conduct disorder. Many young children with ODD left untreated will eventually develop conduct disorder. The younger the onset of ODD, the greater the probability of later developing conduct disorder and being diagnosed with antisocial personality disorder as an adult.

Conduct Disorder

Children with conduct disorder engage in repetitive behavior in which the basic rights of others and/or major age-appropriate societal norms or rules are violated. They are characteristically aggressive to people and animals. They may bully, threaten, or intimidate others; initiate physical fights; use a weapon that can cause serious physical harm to others (such as a bat, brick, broken bottle, knife, or gun); steal while confronting a victim (such as mugging, purse snatching, extortion, or armed robbery); or force someone into a sexual activity.

Another characteristic behavior of children with conduct disorder is destruction of property. Often, they have deliberately engaged in fire setting with the intention of causing serious damage or have intentionally destroyed others' property. A third characteristic of these children is their deceitfulness and thievery. Commonly, they have broken into someone else's house, building, or car; lied or "conned" others to obtain goods or favors or to avoid obligations; or stolen valuable items without confronting a victim (shoplifting or forgery). They have also committed serious violations of rules, such as staying out at night despite parental prohibitions, running away from home and staying overnight, or school truancy.

Obviously, conduct disorder causes clinically significant impairment in family, social, and academic functioning. Further, the prognosis for children with conduct disorder is not encouraging. The earlier the onset of conduct disorder symptoms, the poorer the prognosis and the higher the probability the child will be incarcerated as an adult and experience poor occupational adjustment, marital problems, and social alienation. Treatment for conduct disorder must begin as soon as it is identified and must include family as well as individual interventions.

Attention-Deficit/Hyperactivity Disorder

The central features of attention-deficit/hyperactivity disorder (ADHD) are inattention, hyperactivity, and impulsivity. While many children may demonstrate some of these symptoms on any given day, the child with ADHD will demonstrate many or most of these symptoms consistently starting before they are seven years old, to a degree that is maladaptive and inconsistent with their developmental level, and in more than one setting. Examples of the major symptoms of ADHD are described below.

- *Inattention:* difficulty sustaining attention, does not seem to listen when spoken to directly, often has difficulty organizing tasks and activities, often loses things necessary for tasks or activities, often easily distracted by happenings in the environment, or often forgetful in daily activities.

- *Hyperactivity:* often fidgets with hands or feet, squirms in seat, often runs about or climbs excessively in situations in which it is inappropriate, is often "on the go" or often acts as if "driven by a motor," or often talks excessively.
- *Impulsivity:* often blurts out answers before questions have been completed, often has difficulty awaiting turn, often interrupts or intrudes on others.

Attention-deficit/hyperactivity disorder (ADHD) is notable in this section on disruptive disorders because it is not typically comorbid with depression or bipolar disorder. Some of the symptoms of depression do occur as a result of ADHD because children with this disorder often have social problems and academic failure, leading to feelings of worthlessness. A full depressive or manic episode, however, would not be predicted simply by virtue of having ADHD. This is very interesting in terms of differences between theories of ADHD and theories of depression. Specifically, the neurotransmitters and their mechanisms vary between the two, and there appears to be considerably fewer environmental antecedents of ADHD relative to depression.

Attention-deficit/hyperactivity disorder has been popularized by the media, and many parents and teachers believe they can diagnose it just by spending time with a child. For example, in my practice I am often given referrals in which the parent or teacher says, "I need this child evaluated for ADHD." On the other hand, I hardly ever get referrals in which the diagnosis is presupposed for depression and anxiety, and never for childhood schizophrenia. It is good that people are aware of disorders such as ADHD, but the actual diagnosis and subsequent treatment should be made by a professional with considerable experience differentiating ADHD from other disorders.

Due to the presumption of ADHD in so many children, depression can easily be misidentified as ADHD. Symptoms that overlap between ADHD and depression include sleep difficulties, poor concentration, and agitation. Less frequently, bipolar disorder is misidentified as ADHD. Symptoms that overlap between ADHD and bipolar disorder include hyperactivity and impulsive acting out. When trying to determine whether a child has depression or ADHD, one should consider the family history, patterns of behavior, and age of onset. Children with depression will have parents and grandparents with a history of depression; their overlapping symptoms will look different, and there will be additional depressive symptoms; and the time of onset will probably be later than for ADHD.

SUBSTANCE-RELATED DISORDERS

Substance-related disorders include abuse or dependence on alcohol or other drugs. Types of drugs frequently abused by children and adolescents that cause dependence include amphetamines such as speed, diet pills, crank, crack, or cocaine; caffeine; marijuana; hallucinogens such as LSD or PCP; inhalants such as spray paint, glue, and gasoline; nicotine; heroin; and sedatives. Clinically there is a difference between substance abuse and substance dependence, with dependence being relatively worse than abuse.

Substance Abuse

Substance abuse is a maladaptive pattern of substance use leading to impairment or distress as manifested by:

- recurrent substance use resulting in failure to fulfill major role obligations at home or school (repeated absences, poor school performance, suspensions, or expulsions)
- recurrent substance use in situations in which it is physically hazardous
- recurrent substance-related legal problems
- continued substance use despite having persistent or recurrent social or interpersonal problems caused or exacerbated by the effects of the substance

Substance Dependence

Substance dependence is a maladaptive pattern of substance use leading to clinically significant impairment or distress as manifested by:

- tolerance, a need for markedly increased amounts of the substance to achieve intoxication or markedly diminished effect with continued use of the same amount of the substance
- withdrawal, substance-specific symptoms associated with the immediate cessation of the use of the substance or the use of the substance to avoid the symptoms of withdrawal
- the substance is taken in larger amounts or over a longer period than was intended

- there is persistent desire or unsuccessful efforts to cut down or control substance use
- a great deal of time is spent in activities necessary to obtain the substance
- important life activities are given up or reduced because of the substance use
- the substance use is continued despite knowledge of having a persistent or recurrent physical or psychological problem that is likely to be exacerbated by using the substance

Substance Abuse and Depression

Children begin to abuse alcohol and drugs nowadays as early as eight to ten years of age. Teenagers are much more prone to abuse drugs and alcohol than children, however. For depressed children, drug use may start as a coping mechanism, a technique of getting away, or a method of "self-medicating." Use leads to abuse, and abuse leads to dependence. It is therefore obvious that intervention must begin as early as possible. If a child has been diagnosed with depression at a young age, there is a high probability that the child will abuse alcohol or other drugs later. So the treatment of depression should include the development of coping skills to avoid drug and alcohol abuse before it starts.

CHAPTER 5

TREATMENT OF DEPRESSION

It can be very difficult for parents to learn that their son or daughter is depressed. After the shock of realizing that a child is depressed, parents are challenged to find the most appropriate and effective treatment for their child. This chapter is written to help you understand the many aspects of therapy for children with depression. I will discuss the different types of specialists who treat depressed children and how to select a therapist, the different approaches to treating childhood depression, the stages of counseling, the common medications used to treat childhood depression, the different settings in which children are provided treatment, and ideas about navigating through the complex insurance world.

CLINICIANS WHO TREAT DEPRESSED CHILDREN

In the past, more often than not, when a child suffered from difficult times, the typical person to reach out to the child was not a professional trained to counsel children. Often, the first person to be aware of a depressed child was a friend or a family member. Others who may have aided the child were teachers, other school personnel including counselors and nurses, neighbors, and clergy.

Today, the people in the lives of children with problems appear to be less and less available to them. Often, a child's peers may be more available than these traditional sources of support, but they may have as many problems as the child seeking support. With the prevalence of dual-income parents, single parents, and blended families, today's nuclear and extended families struggle to provide the same support that families did little more than a generation ago. Teachers and school personnel face increasing job demands, removing them more and more from the close and attentive role they had served in the past. The clergy, once a bastion of support to children in need, have been rendered less available in their caregiving role as fewer families participate in organized religion. The combined effect of these changes in the support systems available to a depressed child has increased the likelihood that a professionally trained specialist will be involved in the treatment of a specific child's depression. For this reason, it is very important that parents know the types of therapists who treat childhood depression, how therapy is supposed to occur, and how to find a qualified therapist. The informed parent also needs to understand the different approaches to treating childhood depression, the different therapeutic settings, and how to navigate within the complex health-care system.

It is generally agreed that a program of counseling and medication is the most appropriate and effective approach to treating depressed children. Treating depression through counseling alone, without medication, can be slow and incomplete. Although the child and family may avoid a perceived stigma associated with using antidepressant medications, by not introducing these drugs early in treatment, the period of time the child is at risk for failure and self-destructive behavior is extended. For most depressed children, counseling can effectively treat developmental and cognitive aspects of depression in the long run, but children frequently need the relatively quick treatment gains that antidepressants offer in the short run.

On the other hand, for most depressed children, the practice of prescribing antidepressant medications without counseling is equally insufficient. Although it is oversimplified to say that medications only treat the symptoms, it is easy to understand that medications alone do not teach the child new and more effective ways to cope with and modify the stresses that led the child to be depressed. For these reasons, the most effective approach to the treatment of childhood depression includes both counseling and medication.

The practitioners who treat depressed children are both nonmedical and medical in their orientation. Nonmedical practitioners include counselors, social workers, and psychologists. In addition to these practitioners, there are numerous types of physicians (family physicians, pediatricians, and psychiatrists) who treat childhood depression from a medical or biological perspective. Some psychiatrists provide psychotherapy as well as medication.

There are several distinctions between physicians and nonphysician practitioners. The clearest distinction between these groups is that a physician is a medical doctor and, by virtue of this status, may prescribe medication. They assess the child, prescribe medication, and then follow up with the child within a few weeks to evaluate the effectiveness of the medication at ameliorating the symptoms of depression.

Nonphysician practitioners involved in treating childhood depression also assess the child, but they tend to see the child and the causes of the child's depression from a different perspective. Rather than emphasizing the biological causes of a child's depression, the nonmedical practitioner seeks understanding through examining a number of factors, including the child's personal history, the dynamics of the family, school events, and peer relations, to name a few. In contrast to a physician's primary use of medication to treat a child's depression, the nonmedical practitioner relies on psychotherapy to effect change. We will now look more closely at the various professionals trained to treat depressed children and offer some general guidelines on selecting a clinician.

Nonmedical Practitioners

As noted earlier, there are several different nonmedical professionals who treat depressed children. These include counselors, social workers, and psychologists. In some ways, these practitioners have much in common. For example, they seek to identify similar sources of a child's depression, such as traumatic experiences, family difficulties, school stress, and impaired peer relations. In turn, they share a common form of treatment, referred to somewhat interchangeably as counseling or psychotherapy. Generally, psychotherapy with depressed children occurs in one or more of three modalities: individual psychotherapy, group psychotherapy, and family therapy. We will discuss these modalities in detail later.

Before describing the training and orientation of these various professionals, it is important to recognize that I am painting these professions with a very wide brush. These descriptions should help parents become more familiar with the kinds of practitioners who care for depressed children, but they are only general statements. For example, although there are general training guidelines for a particular type of specialist, there is considerable variation from one practitioner's training to another. Further, one should note that the most important factor in successful therapy with children is the collection of attributes (intelligence, temperament, knowledge, training, motivation, charisma, and so on) the therapist brings to the counseling relationship. Although training in specific approaches is invaluable, without a dynamic and effective person in the therapist's chair, counseling may not be effective.

Counselors

The term *counselor* is a generic name for an individual who counsels and gives advice or assistance to another person. As a professional group, mental health counselors have a relatively recent history. Though some individuals identified themselves as counselors before World War II, it was out of a need for postwar counseling that the field emerged. It is in part due to its relative youth as a profession that counselors, as a group, are poorly defined.

In an effort to increase the professional role of counselors, the American Counseling Association (ACA) and the National Board of Certified Counselors (NBCC) have worked for a number of years to set standards for the training and practice of counselors. Many state legislatures have adopted the standards set by these organizations, and, in most states, the minimum requirement necessary for a counselor to practice independently is Certified Professional Counselor (CPC). To be a CPC, the counselor must have completed a specific program of graduate-level course work in a college approved by the ACA and the NBCC. In order to be certified, counselors typically complete supervised course work in individual, group, marital, and family therapy. Because of the breadth of skills required, it is most common for a counselor to specialize in a particular population (for example, children, adolescents, or adults), modality (individual, group, marital, or family), and approach (such as gestalt, behavioral, or cognitive therapy). In addition to this training, the counselor must successfully complete an examination administered by the NBCC. Finally, the counselor must provide evidence of continuing education in the field of counseling. Although a person can say she is a counselor without meeting these requirements, it is fraudulent and illegal to represent oneself as a Certified Professional Counselor unless the aforementioned standards are met.

Social Workers

Although the social work profession predates counseling by fifty years, its history and professional niche is quite similar to that of counselors. It is not uncommon for social workers to be called counselors. Like counselors, social workers vary based on training, orientation, and individual characteristics.

Some social workers are distinguished from counselors by virtue of their training in identifying and providing community-based resources, such as welfare and social service agencies. Although some social work programs emphasize this training, most emphasize teaching their students counseling skills. This distinction between counselors and social workers is further blurred by the fact that many professionals, including counselors, psychologists, and physicians have, out of necessity, developed the skills to identify and access community-based social resources.

Just as counselors have worked to enhance their role within the broader community by advocating legislation to regulate themselves, so have social workers. With the support of the National Association of Social Workers (NASW), most states have adopted legislation specifying the training necessary to become certified or licensed as a social worker. As with counselors, social work certification requires specific graduate-level training approved by NASW, successful completion of a nationally administered social work examination, and continuing education. In addition to certification at the state and national levels, social workers can obtain an advanced credential of Certified Independent Social Worker (CISW). Thus in many ways, the training and practice of social workers and counselors are indistinguishable.

Psychologists

Of the nonmedical practitioners qualified to work with depressed children, none go through more training than psychologists. While counselors and social workers attend about 45 to 60 semester hours of graduate-level training, psychology programs can require more than 100 semester hours. In addition to these years of classroom learning, psychologists are required to participate in fieldwork, a one-year internship, and a one-year postgraduate residency. After completing these tasks, in order to be licensed, the psychologist candidate is required to successfully complete both written and oral examinations approved by the American Psychological Association (APA). Each state has a Board of Psychologist Examiners whose purpose includes monitoring the practice of psychologists and safeguarding the community. The practice of psychology is protected by state laws and regulations administered by each state's professional licensing board. Some psychologists receive recognition in an area of specialty through diplomat status through the American Board of Professional Psychology (ABPP). Diplomats of the ABPP have demonstrated expertise and specialization in a particular area of psychology, such as clinical psychology or school psychology.

General Guidelines for Selecting a Therapist

As discussed, there are considerable differences in training and approach across practitioners. As you begin to examine the approaches of different therapists, you may be struck by how much they disagree about what is the most effective treatment for childhood depression. Also, you may find that, although many practitioners accept children as clients and patients, relatively few of them have received formal training in the treatment of children. Most therapists, including some who work primarily with children, received their formal training in conducting therapy with adults and have accepted children as clients over time, with only continuing education training in child development and treatment.

Good child therapists are hopeful, enjoy being in children's worlds, can create a sense of security, are nonjudgmental, can be playful, are flexible, can be innovative and creative with space and materials, and are talented at getting access to children's thoughts and feelings. Comfort with the modalities of talking, play, games, role-playing, art, skill building, and sports activities also is helpful. It is important for a counselor to be able to engage in the art of counseling while at the same time being informed by the science of counseling.

Effective counselors need to demonstrate a number of skills, including empathy, regard, respect, and caring for other persons, as well as listening, reflecting, confronting, informal and formal assessment skills, interviewing skills, consultation skills, a capacity to effectively and empathetically provide feedback, and limit-setting abilities.

Besides these characteristics, counselors of children need to possess a core body of knowledge to be effective practitioners. Areas of knowledge should include childhood development, theoretical models for counseling, knowledge of the research and clinical literature about children, familiarity with children's play and play therapy, psychopharmacology, and professional ethics.

It is also important for therapists to be knowledgeable about the clinical and research literature available on treatment guidelines for childhood depression. There are reference materials available that specifically address prevalence, specific features, etiology, and treatment guidelines for children who are depressed. Counselors should have available literature on children's reactions, adjustment, and recovery in relation to such life stresses as loss, abuse, and handicaps. Children dealing with these issues are likely counseling candidates. There is a growing body of research findings on the effects of life events as stressors that negatively affect children's development. The qualified child counselor should be familiar with the literature on the effects of death, divorce, single-parent homes, stepfamilies, child sexual abuse, and drug abuse, to name a few.

Practitioners in the medical community are increasingly treating childhood depression with medication. It is important that clinicians counseling these children have a working knowledge of the effects of medication on children, how they can be used as an adjunct to counseling, and how to help children understand and be in compliance with medication regimens. When considering whether to allow a practitioner to counsel your child, investigate whether he has the qualities and skills mentioned above. Either speak directly with the practitioner about her training or consider a recommendation from someone you trust, who is familiar with the person, and who does not benefit financially from making the referral. Consider contacting the appropriate state regulating agency or a local psychiatric hospital for a referral.

To effectively choose a clinician, several additional things need to be considered, such as the provider's credentials and competence, and if you are comfortable with the professional. You may want to ask about the clinician's area of expertise; what types of treatment are used (medication, therapy, and so on); fee schedules; whether the clinician is certified or licensed; and how long she has been in practice.

The first step to seeking mental health treatment can often be difficult. Some recommendations for your first step include:

- Ask for a referral from your family physician, a friend, or a family member.
- Consult your insurance company to see which professionals are covered by your insurance plan.
- Contact a local mental health center, which usually accepts several insurance plans or works on a sliding scale.
- Inquire at your church.
- Call a local school or university psychiatry or psychology department.
- Contact a local mental health association or another mental health agency.

Medical Practitioners

The typical training for a physician includes baccalaureate preparation for the study of medicine, a university-based medical school, and direct clinical experience as part of medical education. Physicians train for three to seven years beyond medical school, depending on their specialty choice. The specialties that commonly treat childhood depression are family practice, pediatrics, and psychiatry. Because of the breadth of medical practice and the rapid development of new medical information facing physicians, it is expected that these practitioners are dedicated to lifelong learning.

Given the important role the physician may play in your child's welfare, it is vital that you find one with whom you are comfortable. Although we are not accustomed to questioning physicians because of their elevated status in our society, it is a fair and responsible act to investigate the background of a specific physician before agreeing to engage in a professional relationship. Here are some questions you may want to ask: What medical school did the physician attend? Is the physician licensed to practice in your state? If in doubt, call the state medical licensure board to check on the physician's credentials. Where did the physician do her specialty training after graduation? Does the physician have another area of expertise?

Another question is whether the physician is board certified in her area of expertise. Board certification means that the physician has taken advanced training, passed additional written and oral examinations, and regularly attends continuing education classes. Have there been any complaints or actions taken against the physician in any of the states in which he is licensed? Ask about where the physician has hospital privileges, then call the hospital and ask in what area of specialty she works. Hospitals usually will not grant privileges to physicians who do not have the required training. If the physician has no hospital affiliation, find out why. Is the physician an active member of a medical society and, if so, which one?

You may want to consider the following other factors when evaluating your prospective physician's practice. The importance of each element will vary from one individual to another. Is the office conveniently located, easily accessible, orderly, and efficient? Is the physician's office staff friendly and helpful or disorderly and overworked? Are the office medical personnel adequately trained? Will you be seeing the physician, his assistant, or a nurse-practitioner? If the physician has associates, would they be acceptable in an on-call situation? Does the physician seem amiable and knowledgeable? Are you comfortable in her presence and confident with her advice? This information may not guarantee that you will find the doctor who is right for you, but it is certainly a way to narrow your choices. With matters of your family's health, these are questions to which you deserve to have answers.

DIFFERENT APPROACHES TO TREATING CHILDHOOD DEPRESSION

Psychotherapy and Counseling

There are several aspects to counseling children that distinguish the experience from counseling adults. First, children are unlikely to seek help voluntarily or to initiate entry into counseling. When a counselor asks a child, "What brings you in today?" a common reply is, "my Mom." Generally, when adults seek counseling they are motivated to explore their world and make changes. In contrast, the child client may have little idea about why he is brought to the office and may not be motivated to be in therapy or, worse, may be actively opposed to being there.

Second, many children lack an understanding of counseling, the purpose and goals of treatment, and the role they are to assume, in part because they did not initiate help and in part because they are too immature to understand it. Children may not comprehend that they are to share about themselves, gain insight, and change behaviors. It is difficult for them to grasp the purpose and goals of counseling and, as a result, fail to "buy into" the experience.

A third way that children differ from adults in therapy is that a child's verbal and cognitive abilities are not fully developed.

Typically, the preteen child operates on a developmental level that makes it difficult to comprehend subtle psychological concepts. Developmental psychologists refer to preteen children as functioning on a concrete level of cognitive development. For example, preteen children identify the physical attributes of others as their most salient features. When describing a friend they tend to offer physical attributes, physical possessions, or simple personality traits, such as "nice" or "funny." Many forms of counseling demand that the patient gain insight into her own inner world and the inner world of others. Generally, it is not until a person becomes a teenager that she begins to function at the more abstract level necessary for these types of insight-oriented therapy.

A fourth aspect that distinguishes children from adults in counseling is that children are much more dependent on and influenced by their immediate environments, particularly their families, teachers, and friends. Because of the role the immediate environment plays in the life of a child, it is very common for the therapist to interact with and consult parents and teachers in developing a comprehensive plan for the child's success. Although these characteristics of children may appear to be limitations, they also can be viewed as opportunities for practitioners to educate the adults in children's lives as well as the children themselves about the potential benefits of counseling, to work with children early in their personality development, and to influence parents while they are still energized, motivated, and committed.

A final distinction between counseling children and adults is the issue of confidentiality, the understanding that communications between the professional and the client will be private within the limits of the law. Adults understand that what they say will remain confidential and that what they tell their therapists will not be disclosed unless they are a danger to themselves or others or admit to specific illegal actions such as child abuse. In contrast to an adult's limited confidentiality, a child, being a minor, typically has no confidentiality. Parents or guardians have the right to access their children's counseling records. Obviously, this presents a problem for counseling children. A child is quick to detect a breach of confidence if a parent changes her own behavior based on information disclosed in counseling between the child and the therapist. If the child suspects that the therapist is revealing the content of the sessions to his parents, chances are he will be inhibited about revealing sensitive information in the future. Obviously, if this happens, the quality and integrity of counseling is limited and the child's treatment is affected. To solve this problem, parents are often asked to sign a statement that they retain the right to information about the child's counseling, but that they respect the privacy necessary for the child to develop trust with the therapist and, therefore, they will not ask the therapist to disclose details about what the child reveals unless absolutely necessary. As a result, parents are reassured that the child's therapist holds the same interest in the child's welfare and that the therapist agrees to the same expectations regarding confidentiality afforded to an adult.

A primary goal of counseling the depressed child is to assist the child in solving emotional, behavioral, and interpersonal problems that are impinging on his ability to function successfully in the world. The counseling relationship provides the child with a secure base from which to explore his world and to make changes.

Counseling children usually involves counseling and educating the child's parents as well. The relationship the therapist establishes with the child's parents also can provide them with a secure base from which to explore their relationship with the child, including attitudes toward, influences on, and reactions to the child. An open and trusting relationship with the child's parents fosters their motivation to engage in and support change for the child and themselves. As such, the child is seen as the primary client, with secondary relationships established with the child's parents.

Typically, counseling consists of a clinical hour (forty-five to fifty minutes) in a private, quiet office where interruptions are held to a minimum. In counseling, consistency in time and physical location symbolizes the psychological safety and security being offered to the child. Consistency conveys a sense of respect for the child and the counseling process. The counselor's office should welcome children and promote safety and security. The office should contain materials and toys that allow for the expression of feelings. Many therapists provide paper, crayons, markers, scissors, clay, puppets, dolls, games, stuffed animals, building blocks, plastic animals, and a dollhouse. In addition, some therapists provide a small library of children's books related to childhood stresses, such as divorce, death, families, and peer relations.

Individual counseling with children is an ongoing process of planned interactions between a counselor and a child needing help for a particular problem or set of problems. By accepting the child as a client, the therapist agrees to attempt to help alleviate the child's distress and to improve the child's psychological functioning. The therapist is committed to facilitating change in the child and the child's environment, including the school and family.

The counselor begins by developing a strong relationship with the child and the parents. Within this relationship, the practitioner uses techniques that allow for expression, self-examination, building new skills, and promoting better ways to adapt. From the basic trusting relationship the child can explore herself and learn and practice new ways of feeling, thinking, and behaving. By working together with the therapist, the child may develop healthier adaptations and more effective strategies for dealing with difficult situations.

From a basis of trust with the parents, the therapist promotes a new understanding of the child, support for change in the child, and a commitment to examination and change within the adults themselves. Therapeutic techniques are chosen to fit the particular needs of the child and family. Modalities for working with children are many and include verbal interactions, such as talking, storytelling, and dialogue during play; action play; game playing; work with art materials; and use of books and journals. Social skills, including cooperation, assertion, responsibility, empathy, and self-control are taught and monitored in therapy. To assist the development and maintenance of these skills, the therapist trains the child in self-monitoring and self-management techniques. Perhaps the most important concern in counseling is the degree to which the child regularly applies skills acquired in the counselor's office in the real world. Including parents in counseling helps to monitor the generalization or transfer of these skills to home, school, and community settings.

There are many ways of looking at the counseling process. To provide you with a "road map," a six-stage sequence of individual counseling with children is presented here. For simplicity, the counseling process has been divided into stages; however, boundaries between stages may not be evident in practice and the process may not be quite so sequential.

Stage 1: Assessing the Child

When a child is referred for counseling, the therapist evaluates the reason for the referral. Often this assessment involves a review of the child's school and medical records and information from the referral source about the reason for referral. The therapist tries to identify what the problem is and what steps have already been taken to alleviate it. In addition to identifying the nature of the problem, the therapist assesses the appropriateness of the referral and decides whether counseling is needed. If counseling is recommended, the therapist may want to augment individual therapy with family therapy, parent training, or group counseling. The counselor may also consider a plan to involve school personnel. These recommendations are determined, in part, by the nature and degree of severity of the problem the child is exhibiting. Although this informal assessment may provide enough information to determine the child's need for individual counseling, often formal assessment is necessary. Formal assessment of depression is covered in chapter 2.

During this first stage, the child's parents or guardians give information and, if the decision is made to pursue counseling, provide their permission for it. At this time, the counselor clarifies the role of the parents in counseling and how the child's progress will be communicated to them throughout the course of treatment. The initiation of counseling can be understood as a sort of contract. The child presents with a set of problems, and the counselor, the child, and the child's parents agree to engage in a set of activities with the purpose of resolving the problems.

Stage 2: Developing Goals and Planning Interventions

Information that was gathered through the assessment provides the basis for understanding the child's needs and the goals for therapy. At this point, the therapist contemplates the child's depression from a variety of theoretical orientations. This broad perspective allows the therapist several hypotheses about the underlying causes of the depression. From these hypotheses, the therapist develops goals and interventions for the child. The goals and methods chosen need to match the child's cognitive and emotional development. For example, the difficulty that young children have in taking another person's point of view or understanding abstract concepts must be considered when the goals and interventions are formulated.

Specific goals for the child may include lessening depression, anger, or anxiety; improving self-concept, interpersonal skills, or impulse control; or developing appropriate alternative behaviors for situations causing the child distress. Goals may be developed to assist the child within the school environment and at home. These goals may require teachers' and parents' participation by adjusting their approach to the child. They may be asked to change schedules, monitor the child's progress, or provide feedback and rewards to the child in their respective settings.

Stage 3: Beginning Counseling

The primary work at Stage 3 involves preparing the child for counseling. At this point, the counselor gets the child ready for counseling by asking the child about her understanding of and feelings about it. Often children do not comprehend the counseling experience, and the counselor must explain the roles, processes, and purposes of counseling to the child. It is important to use developmentally appropriate language with the child. Preparing the child in this way increases his understanding, cooperation, and investment in the experience.

It is important to consider the child's needs. The counselor should involve the child in the planning process and instill an expectation of hope. The child should know that counseling involves working together to remedy matters that are troubling her. One way to increase a child's involvement in counseling is to provide her with feedback from the assessment. For example, the counselor should review the information shared by parents and teachers regarding depressive symptoms in order to convey a sense of understanding and concern. Any such feedback must consider the child's developmental level, cognitive functioning, and emotional needs.

Also at this stage, guidelines concerning confidentiality need to be explained to everyone involved. Different counselors adopt different policies regarding this issue. For example, some share information with parents concerning the child's general progress while striving to keep the specific content of the counseling sessions confidential. Other counselors inform the child that the parents will have access to information from sessions, but agree to respect the confidentiality of any information the child specifically requests be kept private. Whatever policy is adopted, the counselor, child, and parents must understand that the parents have legal rights to information about their children and that the counselor has a legal obligation to take appropriate action if there is a threat of harm to the child or others.

Sometimes during the beginning phase of counseling the therapist discusses limits and rules with the child, such as time and length of sessions and rules about the use of toys. The child should not be overwhelmed with a long list of rules, nor should a set of rules be imposed before the child feels at ease with the counselor. Often, limits are understood more easily and accepted better when they are discussed as the occasion for them arises.

Stage 4: Working with the Child and Implementing the Plan

A central tenet of counseling is the development of the counselor-client relationship. This relationship provides the foundation for improvement and meeting the counseling goals. In order for progress to be made, a base of trust and security in the counseling relationship must be built. Effective counselors listen with empathy, make emotional connections by striving to see and feel the child's world, communicate that understanding, and offer emotional support to the child. In this trusting relationship, the child can examine threatening feelings and thoughts and can attempt new ways of thinking, behaving, and relating. A counselor's genuine personal warmth and comfort with children will help establish the conditions necessary for building a relationship of trust.

While developing a working relationship with the child, the plan for effecting change is implemented. The qualities and skills used to build this relationship remain relevant throughout the course of counseling. Child counselors use a variety of skills, including a balanced sense of humor, appropriate and relevant self-disclosure, interpretations of the content of what the child discloses to make connections among patterns and themes in the child's life, and confrontation of discrepancies when necessary. During the working phase of counseling, the counselor uses a variety of techniques to address and alleviate the child's depression. These techniques vary depending on the needs of the child and the orientation of the counselor but may include working through skills training, journaling, bibliotherapy, or other therapeutic homework.

Stage 5: Continue Counseling and Modify the Plan as Needed

During the course of counseling, a reevaluation of the original plan, goals, and progress to date may be necessary. Often new information is revealed during counseling that was not disclosed during the assessment because the child and parents now feel more comfortable with the counselor. Sometimes the child's circumstances change during counseling, such as increased marital stress in the family or revelation that the family has little tolerance for the child's behaviors. Periodically during the course of counseling, feedback about the progress of the interventions needs to be given to the child and the parents. Feedback should be provided in an honest but compassionate way. The intent of the feedback is to review areas of improvement and areas that require modification of the original plan to achieve the desired goals. Blaming the child, the parents, or the therapist should be avoided. The purpose of the feedback is to increase the likelihood that the child will benefit from the experience. It is common for the child, parents, and therapist to reevaluate and modify the contract or understanding of the goals of therapy.

Stage 6: Develop a Plan for Termination

In theory, the decision to terminate counseling should be easy. Counseling should end when goals have been met and the child's functioning has improved and stabilized. In practice, the decision to end counseling is seldom simple or ideally planned. Partially met goals, lack of cooperation by significant persons in the child's life, a family move to another city, or the therapist's move to another job may cut short counseling. If the goals have been partially met, enough progress may have been made so that interactions between the child and parents are healthier, thus creating an environment likely to support continued progress. To determine whether progress toward meeting goals has occurred, the therapist may review the present-ing problem and original goals for therapy.

In planning for termination, it is important for the counselor to be sensitive to the significance that the counseling relationship has for the child. Negative feelings, such as anger and sadness, may be evident at the termination of this meaningful relationship. For some children, the end of counseling may reopen feelings associ-ated with earlier separations and losses. These feelings are common and normal. Adequate time during the final counseling sessions should be taken to discuss feelings associated with ending the counseling relationship. Also, attention should be paid to positive feelings associated with the child's improvement and plans for the future. Reassurances that the child will be remembered is impor-tant. Sometimes the child and counselor exchange keepsakes such as photographs, artwork, or stories. Gradual reduction of counsel-ing time may be a helpful way to make the transition. For this rea-son, it is routine to decrease sessions from weekly, to bimonthly, to an as-needed basis. Parents and children should be reassured that they can seek the assistance of the therapist occasionally as a "booster" or "tune-up."

TYPES OF PSYCHOTHERAPY

There are numerous distinct types of psychotherapy used with depressed children. Each type has its own theoretical basis and set of techniques. In this section I provide a cursory overview of the main forms of psychotherapy, including psychodynamic or insight-oriented, behavioral, and cognitive therapy. Developmental aspects of counseling and play therapy are also discussed.

Insight-Oriented Therapy

Psychodynamic therapy and its numerous derivative forms share a common goal of providing insight into unconscious motives and needs that influence behavior. A major assumption of insight-oriented therapies is the notion that our behavior is influenced by forces not immediately available to our conscious mind and that by gaining insight into these needs and motives, the child can be taught more effective ways of responding to them. A simple example of this phenomenon might be a child's jealousy of the attention given to a new addition to the family. The child may present symptoms of depression. Through insight-oriented therapy the child and parents may gain a sense of the importance of the child's need for attention. With this new insight, the child and family can work together to increase the attention given to the child, alleviating the depressive symptoms. Psychodynamic techniques with children include play therapy, reflection of feelings, clarifying, summarizing, and confronting inconsistencies. Using these techniques, the therapist encourages the child to express, elaborate, and become more aware of her feelings.

Behavioral Therapy

Just as insight-oriented therapy has its various forms, behavior therapy is comprised of numerous techniques. Unlike the psychodynamic therapists' emphasis on emotions and insight into unconscious needs and motives, the behavioral therapists assume that behaviors tend to be a function of the antecedents (triggers) and consequences (payoffs) of behavior. Behavioral therapists assert that childhood depression may be the result of a child not feeling in control of how to obtain rewards, such as good grades, peer acceptance, or parental approval. The child believes, "Try as I might, no matter what I do, I won't succeed." This sense of helplessness results in apathy, which results in fewer attempts or less effort to obtain rewards. Once the child has given up, the rewards come less and less. The goal of behavior therapy is to assist the child in finding ways to obtain the desired goals and to regain a sense of mastery and competence. Behavioral approaches include systematic desensitization of fearful situations, assertion training, modeling new and effective behaviors, shaping behaviors by rewarding appropriate behaviors in the sessions, direct instruction of social skills, and self-monitoring of specific behaviors.

Cognitive Therapy

Cognitive therapy is a popular approach to treating childhood depression. Cognitive therapists believe that faulty thinking causes depression. By listening closely to the child, the cognitive therapist seeks and detects distortions, misinterpretations, and overreactions on the part of the child that may lead to depressing interpretations. For example, a child may interpret a close friend's decreased phone calls as rejection. The therapist helps the child by suggesting alternative interpretations of the friend's behavior that may be less depressing, such as a friend being grounded. The therapist also teaches the child to reinterpret events in ways that lead to healthier functioning. Some of the techniques used by cognitive therapists include countering negative thoughts (for example, changing the self-statement "I can't learn math" to "I can do some math, but I am having trouble learning fractions"), anticatastrophic reappraisals (teaching the child to resist the urge to jump to the worst possible scenario and to be more realistic about possible outcomes), label shifting (for example, looking at the glass as half full rather than half empty).

Developmental Perspective

Counseling children demands an understanding of child development, regardless of the counselor's therapeutic orientation. At this time there are several different theories of childhood development, but no single universally accepted view. Knowledge of the various developmental theories and frameworks enhances the practitioner's understanding of the child and his behavior. For example, Freud's psychodynamic theory offers an understanding of the child's underlying needs and motives. Erik Erikson's psychosocial theory enlightens the therapist to the child's search for mastery over specific psychosocial crises. From Jean Piaget, the practitioner gains a sense of the cognitive capabilities and limitations of a child at a particular age. Social learning theorists, such as Albert Bandura, tell us how the child learns through modeling and observation. Attachment theorists, such as John Bowlby, teach us about the importance of attachment, particularly between the child and the mother. Ecological psychologists, such as Urie Bronfenbrenner, enrich our understanding of the transactions between the child and multiple environmental systems. Lev Vygotsky and the contextual psychologists offer insights into the reciprocal influence between the child and parent on defining the world of the child. Knowledge of these multiple perspectives produces a powerful understanding of children's development and the forces that affect the child. The therapist uses this knowledge to conceptualize the child's depression. In turn, the developmental perspective leads to the choice of goals and interventions by matching the process of counseling to the child's developmental levels.

Play Therapy

Because it is a treatment approach used almost exclusively with children, play therapy needs to be reviewed in any discussion of the treatment of childhood depression. Some therapists believe that play is the medium of expression for children. Play to a child is what talking is to an adult. Unlike adults, children may not discuss their feelings but may act them out. Play is natural and comfortable for children. Thus, play can be the natural medium of counseling with children. Play therapy does not belong to a particular theoretical orientation. It is a way to get children to express themselves. Play therapy is used by practitioners of various theoretical orientations including insight-oriented, cognitive, and developmental. Play therapy has been particularly effective in work with traumatized children and children in crisis.

Children use play to work through and master psychological difficulties of the past and the present. From children's play a therapist can learn how a child sees the world and what the child's concerns and problems are. Through play, children express what they cannot put into words. Children typically do not play spontaneously only to pass time; their inner processes, desires, problems, and anxieties motivate how children choose to play. It is essential that a counselor working with children respect their need for expression through play. The presence of toys tells children that the office is a place for them, that they are understood there, and that they can therefore relax and be children. Through play the counselor builds a therapeutic relationship, which becomes the basis for goal identification, interventions, and resolution of problems.

MEDICATIONS USED TO TREAT CHILDHOOD DEPRESSION

As stated earlier, it is becoming increasingly common to treat childhood depression with medication. Whether medication is warranted is ultimately the decision of a physician, such as a family practice physician, a pediatrician, or a psychiatrist. Usually the decision to use medication is based on the severity and longevity of the symptoms and the inability to alleviate the symptoms through counseling.

There are several types of medications that physicians use to treat the symptoms of depression. Each of these medications has different dosages, benefits, and side effects. Antidepressant medications can be categorized into three broad groups: tricyclic antidepressants (TCAs), selective serotonin reuptake inhibitors (SSRIs), and monoamine oxidase inhibitors (MAOIs). A brief discussion about the natural remedy, St. John's wort, is also provided.

Tricyclic Antidepressants (TCAs)

Tricyclic antidepressant medications (TCAs) have been used to treat depressed people since the 1950s. The development and use of TCAs have been considered by some as one of the most significant contributions to psychiatry in the last fifty years. There are a number of TCAs that are commonly prescribed for the treatment of depressed children, including amitriptyline (Elavil), doxepin (Sinequan), trazodone (Desyrel), imipramine (Tofranil), desipramine (Norpramin), nortriptyline (Pamelor), and clomipramine (Anafranil).

TCAs are characterized by their lag in clinical response. Typically, there is a delay of several weeks between beginning a TCA regimen and the initial relief from depressive symptoms. This delay in response is in part because of the common practice of titrating the dosage of medicine, beginning with a small dose and gradually increasing it, to reduce the risk of side effects that might occur if the full therapeutic dose were given initially. A full trial consists of giving the maximum daily dosage for at least two weeks. To reach the maximum dose, the trial encompasses a total of about four to six weeks. It is routine for the physician to conduct a plasma level; that is, to draw blood to determine whether there is a sufficient amount of medication in the child to achieve a therapeutic benefit. The most common reason a TCA fails to achieve results is that there has been an insufficient amount of time allowed for the drug to work before the patient quits taking it.

TCAs tend to affect both serotonin and norepinephrine, two neurotransmitters implicated in depression. Because they can have a sedating effect, most TCAs are given in a single dose at bedtime. TCAs typically are not prescribed to children with known cardiac disease or arrhythmia, a family history of cardiac disease, syncope (brief episodes of lightheadedness), or a seizure disorder. While on TCAs, careful attention should be given to pulse, blood pressure, and electrocardiogram.

Unfortunately, TCAs are not perfect in the treatment of depression; about 70 to 80 percent of depressed individuals have the desired response to them. Another shortcoming of TCAs is their various side effects, which result in children prematurely discontinuing medication. Further, the concerns they pose for the heart and for seizures make many families cautious.

Selective Serotonin Reuptake Inhibitors (SSRIs)

A relatively new class of antidepressants, selective serotonin reuptake inhibitors (SSRIs), are appreciated for their effectiveness without the side effects or concerns presented with TCAs and MAOIs. The SSRIs include fluoxetine (Prozac), paroxetine (Paxil), sertaline (Zoloft), nefazodone (Serzone), bupropion (Wellbutrin), venlafaxine (Effexor), and fluvoxamine (Luvox).

SSRIs have shown effectiveness in the treatment of depression, panic attacks, bulimia, and obsessive-compulsive disorders. SSRIs are preferred by practitioners because of their favorable side-effect profile, their relative lack of cardiotoxicity, and their wide margin of safety in overdose situations. Unlike the TCAs, which are sedating and given at night, the SSRIs tend to be activating and are given in the morning, so as not to interfere with sleep. For some individuals, however, SSRIs are sedating and are therefore taken at night. Although there tend to be few side effects with SSRIs, these include headache, nausea, tinnitus, insomnia, and nervousness.

Monoamine Oxidase Inhibitors (MAOIs)

Physicians have used monoamine oxidase inhibitors (MAOIs) to treat depression since the 1950s. The commonly used MAOI is phenelzine (Nardil). The use of MAOIs has never been as common as the use of TCAs because of various side effects including hypotension, tachycardia, sweating, tremor, nausea, and insomnia. Another major drawback to the use of MAOIs is the need for the patient to follow a diet that avoids the consumption of tyramine, an amino acid contained in aged cheeses, meats, bananas, yeast-containing products, and alcoholic beverages. Failure to avoid tyramine when taking an MAOI may result in a hypertensive attack.

In spite of these concerns, when TCAs and SSRIs are found to be ineffective and the individual presents specific symptoms of depression referred to as atypical depression (anxiety, tension, phobias, panic, hysterical features, irritability, mood reactivity, overeating, and oversleeping), MAOIs may be prescribed. For this reason, MAOIs are thought of as the physician's third line of defense for medical treatment of depression.

MAOIs are administered in a gradual stepwise dosage and may be given in the morning or in the evening, depending on their effect on sleep. They tend to be effective at a relatively low dose.

Lithium Carbonate

Lithium is the medication of choice in the treatment of bipolar disorder. Bipolar mood disorder may be characterized by a variety of patterns of extreme highs and lows. Lithium is commonly used to treat children with severe aggression, emotionally unstable children, and depressed children whose parents have responded favorably to lithium. Lithium has also been effective in augmenting the benefit of SSRIs in children with treatment-resistant depression and obsessive-compulsive disorder.

Unlike SSRIs, lithium requires close monitoring when prescribed. Because it is a salt, it is contraindicated for patients with known renal, thyroid, or cardiac disease and those at risk for dehydration and electrolyte imbalance.

Anxiolytics (Anti-Anxiety Agents and Sedatives)

Often, depressed children present symptoms of anxiety, such as panic, muscle tension, and excessive worry. Anti-anxiety medications, anxiolytics, treat anxiety and its symptoms primarily through generalized sedation of the central nervous system. There are numerous anxiolytics, including alprazolam (Xanax), chlordiazepoxide (Librium), clonazepam (Klonopin), clorazepate (Tranxene), diazepam (Valium), lorazepam (Ativan), oxazepam (Serax), buspirone (Buspar), and prazepam (Centrax).

There are a number of adverse side effects that can occur from anxiolytic medications. These include disinhibition, ataxia (impaired motor performance), dysarthria (poorly articulated speech), and nystagmus (involuntary eye movement). Further, cases of agitation, disorientation, mood lability (rapid changes in mood), and amnesia have been reported with some anxiolytics. Overdose with these medications may result in respiratory depression, hypotension (low blood pressure), shock syndrome, coma, and death. Abrupt withdrawal of sedative drugs may cause serious and possibly fatal convulsive seizures. Newer anxiolytics such as Buspar have far fewer side effects.

In spite of these risks, anxiolytics are sometimes necessary to rapidly reduce a child's anxiety levels. A judicious practice commonly used by some physicians it to prescribe anti-anxiety medications briefly until antidepressant medications achieve a therapeutic effect, usually four to six weeks. After the antidepressant medication takes effect, the anxiolytic medication is reduced gradually and then discontinued.

St. John's Wort

St. John's wort is a natural or herbal remedy for depression. Also known as goatweed, St. John's wort grows wild in Chile, the United States, and Europe. It has been used as a treatment for dysthymia, mild depression, and anxiety since the 1930s. At this time, approximately eighteen double blind studies have been conducted on the effectiveness of St. John's wort for treating depression. These studies have shown it to be safe and effective for treating depression with few side effects. Currently, the derivative of St. John's wort used to treat depression is called hypericin. This may not be the only effective component of St. John's wort. Other derivatives such as hyperfolin are being studied, and some researchers think that a combination of all the derivatives of St. John's wort would be most effective.

The most prominent side effect is photosensitization (oversensitivity to light), especially in fair-skinned individuals. St. John's wort should not be eaten raw and should only be taken in capsule or liquid form produced by respectable companies in standardized dosages. St. John's wort is a highly popular treatment for depression in Germany, where it is available only by prescription but prescribed much more often than antidepressant drugs such as SSRIs.

St. John's wort is available over the counter in the United States, and as such a few words of warning should be delivered. First, no systematic study has been done on the safety or effectiveness of St. John's wort for children. As with many antidepressant medications used with children, the drug is assumed to work safely and effectively based on research with adults. Currently, a substantial effort is being made to study antidepressants with children. This effort has not yet been applied to St. John's wort, however. Children may require lower doses, and the magnitude of side effects has not been established. Second, one should not start taking St. John's wort without first consulting your physician. There are known interaction effects between St. John's wort and other medications, such as MAOIs, that must be considered. Third, determining the severity of one's depression is a job for the professional, and determining the treatment options most appropriate for the particular type and severity of depression should be determined through consultation with a clinician. You may find that a young person's mild depression may best be treated with St. John's wort rather than an antidepressant medication. You may also find that your child's severe depression may require more aggressive treatment. This decision should not be made without consideration of many variables including a blood workup, clinical diagnosis, and medical monitoring.

TREATMENT SETTINGS

The treatment of childhood depression occurs in a variety of settings, including outpatient therapy in a private office, day or evening programs, residential treatment, and hospitalization. These settings can be understood as existing along a continuum from the least restrictive or least intensive, such as an outpatient office, to the most restrictive or most intensive, such as an acute inpatient hospital setting. Where treatment occurs depends on several factors, including the severity of the depressive symptoms, resistance of symptoms to treatment, the history of treatment, and situations that may interfere with effective treatment in a particular setting.

Outpatient Office

The vast majority of depressed children are treated in outpatient offices. A typical counseling session consists of forty-five to fifty minutes of time that may be shared between the child, the parents, and other family members, as needed. The outpatient office is a quiet, private setting where interruptions are held to a minimum. In these settings, consistency in time and physical location conveys a sense of psychological safety, security, and respect for the child and the counseling process.

Day or Evening Programs

Although most children respond favorably to treatment in an outpatient setting, some children require more intensive treatment modalities than those offered at an outpatient office. Typically, day and evening programs are provided at hospitals and clinics that have the advantage of a team of practitioners. In contrast to the hour of therapy provided at an outpatient office, children participating in a day or evening program receive from three to four hours of therapy, usually three to five days each week. After the treatment day is completed, the child returns home. One advantage of a day or evening program is that the child remains in the home.

Unlike therapy at an outpatient office, which includes predominantly individual counseling, therapy in day or night programs involves a mix of individual and group counseling. The staff at the program provide various activities that often include group therapy, educational groups, expressive therapy groups, and recreational activities. Soon after a child begins a day or evening program, the treatment team meets and develops a treatment plan. The plan specifies the problems, goals, objectives, interventions, and estimated length of treatment. The treatment plan guides therapy and identifies the criteria to be met before the child is discharged from the program. Typically, when a child is discharged from a day or evening program, his care is shifted to an outpatient setting.

Residential Treatment

As the name suggests, residential treatment is distinguished from outpatient, day, or evening programs by virtue of the fact that the child resides at the facility while receiving twenty-four-hour supervision and care. Residential treatment consists of a structured living environment in which strong attachments and commitment by the staff to the child are essential. Special education services are typically provided to children in residential settings.

Staff at a residential treatment center include psychiatrists, nurses, social workers, counselors, and psychologists, making it quite expensive. There also may be other adjunctive therapists, such as art, music, occupational, and recreational therapists. Soon after a child's admission to residential treatment, the team meets to develop a treatment plan for the child. This plan identifies the problems, goals, objectives, interventions, and time frame for the child's treatment. The team communicates from shift to shift and routinely meets to review the child's progress toward specific goals.

Residential treatment facilities are designed to take into account the physical, cognitive, emotional, and educational needs of their residents. Typically, residents share a room with another child of the same sex, and boys and girls are separated into different living quarters. In most facilities, however, daily activities are coeducational.

Residential treatment is not a treatment of first choice. Intensive outpatient efforts, including individual therapy, family therapy, and medications should have been tried before placement in a residential treatment center is considered. To be effective, residential treatment requires placement for several months. It is very common for a child to be on a "honeymoon" when first admitted to a residential program. During this period, a child may present himself in an uncharacteristically positive way, making a novice therapist question the need for residential placement. When the child acts overly positive and symptom free, the parents feel awkward, wondering if the practitioners question why the child is in the program.

One of the primary values of residential treatment is that children recreate their home world at the residential treatment center. That is, they develop the same problematic ways of relating to residential center staff and residents that they did with their parents, teachers, and peers. Although this may be seen at the time as a setback, and the parents and staff may need reassurance, the reality is that before genuine change can occur the child must display the dys-functional behaviors that warranted admission to the program. In some ways, the demonstration of the problem behaviors indicates that the child has relaxed his defenses and is being herself. It is at this point that effective treatment begins.

A major strength of residential treatment is that behavior can be managed twenty-four hours a day, for several months. In outpatient counseling the child may never demonstrate these behaviors, never allowing the counselor, to deal with the behaviors firsthand. Also, on an outpatient basis, the therapist and parents may not be suc-cessful in managing the child's behavior, in effect perpetuating the problem.

Hospitalization

Because acute childhood depression can be volatile, some chil-dren need to be hospitalized in a psychiatric hospital. It is unusual for children to need to be hospitalized for depression. But it is needed when a child is judged to be a danger to self or others, or when the child is so severely disabled that he may be at risk for harm if not hospitalized. The psychiatric hospital team is led by the at-tending psychiatrist and is comprised of psychologists, nurses, counselors, and social workers. There also may be other adjunc-tive therapists, such as art, music, occupational, and recreational therapists.

Within the first few hours after the child is admitted to a psy-chiatric hospital, the psychiatrist and nursing staff evaluate the child and develop a plan. There are several purposes to psychi-atric hospitalizations. The first is to evaluate the child to anticipate her return to the community. Because psychiatric hospitalizations are brief, usually three to seven days, the team is immediately charged with the task of assessing the child for discharge planning. The team works to understand the severity of the symptoms, the factors contributing to the symptoms, resources the child and the family bring to the child's recovery, and the viability or limitations of specific discharge plans.

As they develop these plans for discharge, the team is also working to stabilize the child psychologically. Before the child can be discharged, the severity of depressive symptoms, particularly suicidal ideation and intent, need to be reduced to a level that is safe for the child. Because of the severity and intensity of the depression, medication is commonly initiated in the hospital. The continuous monitoring of the child by nursing staff allows the physician to be more aggressive when medicating the child than can be done on an outpatient basis. The child's response to the medication is observed directly, and notations are made on an hourly basis. Any medication side effects are recorded immediately. If there are concerns, the medications can be reduced, discontinued, or augmented.

Perhaps the most important benefit of hospitalization is the immediate safety the hospital provides for the child. Typically, before a child is hospitalized, the child and the child's family have experienced a prolonged period of distress. Hospitalization provides sanctuary for the child and respite for the child's parents and family. Once stabilized and beyond the immediate risk of harm, the child is discharged from the hospital. Before the discharge occurs, the team and the family work out a detailed discharge plan, including aftercare.

Community Mental Health Services

Community mental health services are an important element in the mix of services available for the depressed child and her family. Community-based mental health services trace their origins to the turn-of-the-century mental hygiene movement. The intent of this movement was to take the practice of public health out of physicians' offices and into the community. Immediately after World War II until the end of the Johnson presidential administration was a period when community mental health flourished. Although it is a broad concept and has many faces, there are common aspects to community mental health.

Community mental health is provided, in part or in full, through taxpayer monies. The community a particular clinic serves is identified by a catchment area, a designated geographic area. The clinic provides comprehensive mental health services to all the eligible individuals within the catchment area. These services include inpatient care, outpatient care, emergency care, partial (day and/or evening) hospitalization, community consultation, and education programs. Some of these services are not provided by the community mental health center; they are contracted by the center to be provided by other agencies. Implicit in this set of services is a continuum of care from the least intensive to most intensive level of service.

One of the strongest features of community mental health programs is the commitment to prevention of mental illness. Community programs believe in a three-pronged approach to prevention. Primary prevention tries to eliminate factors that cause mental illness through consultation and education of the community including teachers, clergy, welfare workers, and probation officers. Secondary prevention is the practice of early identification and treatment of mental illness. This occurs by providing easy access to services for acute situations. The goal of tertiary prevention is the elimination or reduction of residual disability after an illness. Community mental health centers are committed to both prevention and rehabilitation of mental illnesses.

Because many contemporary families do not fall under the umbrella of primary insurance, community mental health centers are becoming more and more important in the array of treatment options. Although their titles vary from state to state, each state and county have available community-based services. To access these services, one needs to contact the local social service or welfare agency. If you call in a nonemergency situation, an appointment will be scheduled during which an evaluator will assess your situation, the services to be provided, your ability to pay for these services, and the percentage of the cost for which you will be responsible. One advantage of community-based services over treatment with an individual practitioner is the range of services available to the child. Typically, community-based services include emergency care and in-home care, two referral services not available from the traditional therapist.

NAVIGATING THE WORLD OF INSURANCE

Traditional Indemnity or Fee-for-Service Insurance

Under traditional fee-for-service insurance, you can choose any licensed physician to be your personal doctor, and you can use the services of any hospital or other health-care facility. In these health-insurance plans, doctors practice independently with little or no assessment of their performance by their peers or government regulators. For most people with traditional health insurance, premiums are only one part of the cost. Consumers must also pay deductibles, coinsurance, and the cost of services that are not covered, such as physicals. In summary, with traditional indemnity plans, the major benefit is an unrestricted choice of provider. The weaknesses of the traditional plans include limited preventive care, claim forms to file, increased cost to the consumer, and little or no coordination of care.

Managed Care

In contrast to care under a traditional indemnity plan, managed-care enrollees receive care that is either provided directly by or authorized by the managed-care plan. Usually, you may choose your primary care physician from a list of available doctors. If you don't make a choice, the plan will assign you a doctor. Most plans permit you to change primary care physicians if you wish. Your choice of primary care physician is most important. The primary care doctor you choose becomes your personal physician and coordinates your care. She acts as a "gatekeeper," treating you directly or authorizing you to have tests, see a specialist, or enter a hospital. The gatekeeper arrangement is designed to provide the necessary care at the lowest cost and to avoid giving unnecessary care. Managed-care plans usually have quality review procedures that may include internal and external quality assurance programs. For plans that are "federally qualified" or are qualified to provide health care to Medicare or Medicaid enrollees, federal law requires a quality assurance program. Many states have similar requirements. The overall performance of the plan is monitored through government over-sight, patient satisfaction surveys, data from grievance procedures, and independent reviews. The federal government and private quality assurance organizations are developing more sophisti-cated techniques for measuring the quality of care provided by managed care and other organizations and for communicating infor-mation about quality that consumers can use to make informed health-care choices.

Managed-care plans review the medical care proposed by your doctor to determine whether it is appropriate and necessary. This is called a "utilization review." Your primary care physician is part of the utilization review. When hospital care is indicated, other fac-tors and safeguards in the utilization review include preadmission certification, concurrent review, discharge planning, case manage-ment, and second opinions. Preadmission certification is approval for care in advance. Without obtaining approval in advance, the plan may not pay for nonemergency services. Concurrent review is the practice of managed-care plans to monitor your hospital stays to be sure they are no longer than absolutely needed and that all tests and procedures that are ordered are medically necessary. Man-aged-care plans want to keep hospital stays to their shortest appro-priate length. As part of discharge planning, if necessary, the plan will arrange posthospital care, nursing home care, or home health care. Case management is the managed-care practice of developing care plans for complicated cases to be sure care is coordinated and provided in the most cost-effective manner. For example, a plan might provide round-the-clock home care in order to avoid expensive hospital stays. Often, managed-care plans reduce costs by requiring a second opinion before scheduling elective surgery.

The second physician may be asked to judge the necessity of the surgery and also to express an opinion on the most economical, appropriate place to perform the surgery (in a hospital, an outpatient clinic, or a doctor's office).

Several states have enacted laws that prohibit managed-care plans from including so-called "gag clauses" in physician contracts. Gag clauses prevent the plan's doctors from discussing the full range of treatment options with patients, whether or not the plan actually covers the services.

Some managed-care plans give gatekeepers financial incentives to avoid unnecessary referrals to specialists. Because these incentives might discourage doctors participating in a managed-care network from providing needed care, it is critical that managed-care plans be monitored by appropriate outside organizations to ensure that members get the care they need. In the case of Medicare managed-care plans, the Health Care Financing Administration (HCFA) is responsible for this monitoring function.

With managed care, out-of-pocket costs are generally lower, and there is far less, if any, paperwork for beneficiaries to contend with.

Preferred Provider Organizations (PPOs)

Preferred provider organizations offer individuals the choice of staying in or going out of a network of providers for care. Preferred provider organizations contract with physicians and other professionals who provide services to subscribers. Subscribers receive services for a lower cost if providers within the network are used. Subscribers may use providers who are outside their network; however, they pay a higher cost for doing so. Preferred provider organizations require additional paperwork to secure approval for some services. They also coordinate care; however, the amount of coordination is limited compared to managed care or health maintenance organizations.

Health Maintenance Organizations (HMOs)

There are three types of health maintenance organizational models: a staff model, a point-of-service model, and an individual practice association (IPA). An HMO staff model is characterized by a centralized facility where care is provided and coordinated. Typically, HMOs require low copayments compared to other types of health insurance. HMOs were developed on the model of preventive care, with the assumption that it is less expensive to keep the subscribers healthy than to treat ill subscribers. Another benefit of HMOs is that subscribers do not have to bother with claim forms. Individuals who receive services through an HMO must use doctors in the HMO, and the plan must approve treatment and make referrals.

Compared to the staff model HMO, subscribers have more choice of providers outside the network in a point-of-service HMO. Like the staff model HMO, the point-of-service HMO emphasizes preventive care and there are no claim forms. Like the PPO, subscribers pay a higher cost if they prefer to use a provider who is not within the HMO staff, and the plan must sometimes approve treatment and make referrals. Also, out-of-network coverage may be limited.

In the case of the IPA, providers use their own offices to offer services. Like the other types of HMOs, an IPA provides services at a low cost to subscribers and endorses a preventive model of health care, and there are no claim forms. Subscribers use doctors from a designated list, and the plan must sometimes approve treatment and make referrals.

A Checklist to Help You Compare Health-Care Plans

Here are ten important features to consider as you compare different health-care plans.

1. *Benefits*: What is covered by the plan? What is not?
2. *Cost*: What are the costs of the plan? How do the plan rules affect what I pay?
3. *Doctors*: Who are the doctors in the plan? What are their qualifications? Are their offices convenient to me?
4. *Hospitals*: What hospitals are affiliated with the plan? Do they meet my medical needs?
5. *Enrollee satisfaction*: What do enrollees think of their health plan? How many members disenrolled from the plan during the past three years?
6. *Doctor satisfaction*: How many primary care physicians have left the plan during the past three years?
7. *Emergency, urgent, and out-of-area care*: How does the plan handle emergency or urgently needed care? What happens if I am outside the plan's service area?
8. *Accreditation*: Has the managed-care plan been evaluated by an independent accrediting organization?
9. *Complaints*: How does the plan handle complaints? What is the plan's record regarding complaints?

10. *Special features*: What are other special features of the managed-care plans?

Employee Assistance Programs (EAPs)

Employee assistance programs are comprehensive programs designed to provide immediate short-term assessment and support to employees. Often, large companies provide employee assistance internally through their personnel or human resources departments. Smaller companies provide these services by contracting with an independent person or group. This arrangement is referred to as an external EAP.

In either case, certain assumptions compel the company to provide EAP services, and there are certain standards for practice and services provided. Companies provide EAP services because they believe employees are most valuable when they are productive and satisfied with how they manage their home and work lives. When an employee is experiencing serious problems, job performance can suffer. Employee assistance programs are viewed as a cost-effective, humanistic method of assisting employees, their families, and the organization. An EAP may support parents of depressed children and provide referrals for employees and their families, including their children. The EAP's staff helps by working with employees in several other ways. By promoting its counseling services at the workplace through posters, memos, mailings, and orientation, the EAP attempts to identify problems at an early stage. Through early identification, interventions can be more effective and the adverse impact of a problem may be lessened.

An EAP assists employees with their problems directly, or it may assist them in finding available resources. EAPs consult with companies on policy development issues and organizational change to foster healthy work environments. Additionally, they provide educational opportunities through general employee workshops and human resources development for supervisory personnel.

EAPs assist employees with a number of problem areas including marital discord, divorce, drug and alcohol abuse, parenting issues, loss and grief, depression, stress, mental health issues, and children's emotional problems. Typically, their services include employee orientations, confidential assessment and referral, twenty-four-hour telephone assistance, workshops, supervisor and managerial training, consultation, and benefit information. Employees can find out about their EAP by contacting their personnel or human resources departments.

CHAPTER 6

CRISIS MANAGEMENT

Children with emotional problems at times may act drastically. The drastic acts warrant a response from parents and caregivers 100 percent of the time. It is the nature of the response to a crisis, however, that determines its outcome and how frequently the child will exhibit the drastic behavior again. In this chapter we discuss suicide, physical aggression, delinquent actions, and running away. Through understanding the motivations for these drastic actions and how they are related to a child's depressive syndrome, you will be better able to determine the appropriate response to these sometimes frightening and always stressful behaviors.

SUICIDE

Suicide is the act of taking one's own life. Suicide typically happens after much pain and thought. It usually is not the first thing children try to rid themselves of pain, and, therefore, there are opportunities to prevent suicide. It is my hope that by understanding the mind of the child and what to do when you see warning signs, completed suicide will be avoided. I should say at this point that suicide cannot always be avoided, and, if it should occur, you should not blame yourself. In the end, it is an individual decision, rational or not.

Children naturally lack experience in a wide range of ways by virtue of being young. They also may lack sufficient coping skills to contend with new experiences or feelings. For the depressed child, commonly acquired coping skills may never develop despite the efforts of parents. Children suffering from emotional problems seem to lack the sensitivity or motivation to learn all-important coping mechanisms. For example, if a nondepressed child is put down about her ability to play basketball, she will probably recall from her history that she is not all bad. Or she may say to herself that she is just learning, so of course she would not be that good. This is a cognitive or thinking coping skill that most people acquire naturally. The depressed child, however, may simply agree with the rude evaluator. When coping skills break down in a big way, a child may begin to feel worthless, hopeless, and helpless. An easy, but inappropriate, source of coping with such feelings is dying.

The choice to die at this point is not based on an objective understanding of the consequences of the act of suicide. You have probably felt bad after being challenged by an event or person and later realized it was a good learning opportunity and that you gained insight through the challenge. You may even learn that when being challenged, one should look for the learning opportunity and not take the situation personally. Children who want to die do not see things this way. The child who has decided that death is the easiest way out doesn't think about the future, he only thinks about now—and now does not look that good to him. The child begins to send signals that he is not wanting to deal with certain aspects of life. For example, the child may not want to go to school or play her favorite games. More important, associated with avoidance comes direct statements of wanting to die. These statements may be veiled in jokes, or the child may laugh them off. A child may write a note or a poem that includes images of dying, having no future, or feeling helpless.

Wanting to die is an early stage of the process of wanting to commit suicide but is still several steps away from committing the act. The earlier these signs are noticed and the earlier there is a response from a caring adult, the better the outcome will be. After having feelings of wanting to die the child may start to behave in ways that could be considered suicidal; specifically, engaging in risk-taking behavior and, more seriously, after the child has started to develop a plan of how to die, parasuicidal behavior.

Risk-taking behavior can be identified in the words a child says and in his actions. For example, an adolescent who won't wear a seat belt in the car followed by the statement that he doesn't need to wear one because it wouldn't matter if he died from a car accident is a sign of risk-taking behavior. This is pretty obvious, but when it is your own child sometimes you don't want to see the obvious. Risk-taking behaviors include dodging moving vehicles on the road, using high doses of illicit drugs, pointing a gun at oneself, or trying to go too fast in whatever extreme sport in which the child is interested. Taking risks can cause death, and not preventing one's own death is a form of suicide. Many times deaths related to risk taking are considered accidents, but a psychological autopsy would reveal that the child was probably depressed and really wanted to die.

Some children engage in parasuicidal behavior after having contemplated death. Here a child is "dancing" around suicide. This may include making slash marks on the wrist, jumping off low buildings or fences, playing Russian roulette with a loaded weapon, using drugs or alcohol with the hope of overdose, or "trying out" a noose around one's neck. Again, people can die from such acts, although the person may not leave a note behind or directly tell someone that he is going to kill himself. In one family in which the adolescent had threatened suicide, the child and family had been through innumerable treatment options, and emotional distance was continually increasing between the child and the family. This teenager shot himself in the head in the backyard with a shotgun. The family was convinced that he was just cleaning the gun because that was something he had done in the past. This is an example of actual suicide rationalized as an accident. To help the family members understand the actions of the child, they first had to accept the notion of parasuicidal behavior and that cleaning and handling the gun while depressed was just another indication, along with the youth's threats and behavior, that suicide was imminent.

The desire to die as a coping mechanism is not initially associated with a concrete plan of how or when to die. A child is frankly suicidal when she develops a plan, acquires the effective means, and plots a time to commit suicide. Indeed, many suicides are impulsive; the plan and means are in hand, but the time is not premeditated. A professional with training in dealing with crises conducts a suicide assessment on children who threaten to or who have attempted to kill themselves. Identifying if the child has said she wants to die, has developed a plan, has realistic access to the means, and has determined a time to commit suicide are the main questions that should be asked to determine the lethality of a suicidal person. Also, a history of suicide attempts, a history of depression, drug use, and a history of anxiety are all risk factors that increase the probability that a child or, more frequently, an adolescent, will kill herself. Suicide is considered a result of depression and not a symptom. Recurrent thoughts of suicide are a symptom of depression, however.

Incidence of Suicide

The incidence of suicide has more than tripled since 1960. Among children between the ages of ten and fourteen, suicide is the fourth leading cause of death behind unintentional injuries, cancer, and homicide. Among adolescents and young adults between the ages of fifteen and twenty-four, suicide is the third leading cause of death behind unintentional accidents and homicide. Accidental deaths include motor vehicle accidents, and, although there is no hard data, inevitably a percentage of motor vehicle accidents in particular and accidents in general are disguised suicides. For depressed children, research indicates that suicide occurs in about 14 of every 100,000 adolescents, and between 30 and 50 percent have seriously considered suicide. Among identified depressed adolescents, suicide attempt rates range between 8 and 14 percent. Suicide accounts for between 2,000 and 2,500 deaths per year, and there are between 100 and 120 attempts for every death.

Boys complete suicide five and a half times more often than girls, although girls attempt suicide more frequently. This is because boys tend to use quicker and more lethal methods. Two-thirds of completed suicides were done so using a firearm. The second most frequent method is hanging, and third is poison or overdose. When very young children complete suicide, it is often by jumping off of buildings. It is clear that guns and the suicidal adolescent do not mix—if you have a depressed or suicidal child and own a gun, get rid of the gun now. This cannot be overstated; guns effectively kill people, and suicidal adolescents use guns to kill themselves far more than any other means.

Precipitating Events

Adolescents become suicidal for a variety of reasons, most of which have accumulated over the developmental period. Children who attempt suicide typically report specific events that lead them to actually develop a plan. The following are the most frequently reported precipitating events.

Argument with Parents

Arguing with parents is relatively common, and the fact that some children report that it caused them to attempt suicide does not mean that parents should be afraid to argue with their children. Arguing is rarely productive, but at times it is a step along the way to getting an adolescent to express his feelings. There are two specific instances when arguing leads to a suicide attempt. First, if the child is using the suicidal threat during an argument to manipulate the parents, it is easy for the child to threaten suicide and gain control over the parent. In these cases, the parent must take back control by taking the threat seriously and following through on emergency mental health procedures (described later). Letting the threat go and saying the adolescent is just threatening or is just seeking attention is inappropriate; it will lead to more severe threats or actions and may result in a completed suicide.

The second case is when a parent does not finish the argument in a positive way and fails to identify the adolescent's real needs. Having a knock-down drag-out argument with a teenager, then just walking away without reaching a mutual closure, makes the child feel disrespected and misunderstood. This, associated with feelings of worthlessness and hopelessness, results in a real consideration of dying by the child or adolescent.

Breakup of Relationship

A specific loss children and adolescents have little experience with is breakups of their first few relationships. This lack of experience without much parent or peer support can result in feelings of wanting to die. This is exacerbated when the child is also depressed.

Peer Problems

During the school-aged years, social development is fraught with challenges. Particularly frustrating to children is being ostracized by most peers, being rejected by particular peers, and being the object of ridicule. These events exacerbate feelings of loneliness, hopelessness, and worthlessness. Other times, after a child has been able to make friendships, there might be emotionally painful and stressful repercussions when there is a breakup or parting of ways. Some children may be threatened with physical violence by a bully or a gang. Also, a peer might start terrible rumors about the child, thus worsening an already difficult social landscape.

Loss of Loved One

We have discussed that loss at an early age can be a major factor in depression. In older children, loss tends to lead to bereavement and adjustment problems. For the already depressed child with few coping skills, the loss of an important figure in his life or the loss of the only supportive person in his life can be devastating.

Public Humiliation

Particularly for adolescents, public humiliation in the form of being the butt of a public joke (à la Stephen King's *Carrie*) or just making an obvious mistake in a classroom presentation can set off a series of self-deprecating cognitions that the child may be unable to stop. The adolescent may feel he cannot come to school for fear of ridicule or further humiliation.

Problems with Teachers

Teachers represent a major support system for some children. A severe personality conflict with his teachers can result in heightened feelings of disenfranchisement for a depressed adolescent. Some teachers may be insensitive to the highly empathetic and overpersonalizing style of a depressed adolescent and use taunting or ridicule in a joking way. This may be okay for nondepressed teens, but it is very hurtful and causes rumination in the depressed child.

Significant Family Changes

Among the various stressors that can contribute to a child choosing suicide as an option are divorce and moving. These family changes do not cause the suicidal ideations in themselves, but without proper support the depressed child may be unable to cope with such changes. Prior to making significant family changes, it is wise to work with a counselor to help the depressed child manage. This process has been called "stress inoculation" by Donald Meichen-baum. Specifically, the child is reminded about her tendency to make negative self-statements and inaccurate attributions and is taught to make appropriate self-statements and counter irrational beliefs with more rational thoughts.

Myths About Suicide

To be able to talk with a child or adolescent who is suicidal, it is important to understand the myths that have been associated with suicide. The following myths often prevent people from talking can-didly with a suicidal person and contribute to the person's feelings of hopelessness.

It Is Not Inherited or Destined

Some believe that having a suicidal tendency is inherited. Indeed, depression has a genetic link, but this associated suicidal potential in most cases must be associated with significant life stressors to cause an impact. There is no heritability of a suicidal tendency once you have factored out depression. Any correlation between parent and child suicides is accounted for by an underlying emotional prob-lem. Further, research has shown that the biological indicators of suicide are the same as the neurotransmitter (serotonin) and hor-monal (CRF) factors (discussed in chapter 2) shown to cause depres-sion. Movies have popularized the notion that suicide is destined. Images of protagonists grappling with their parents' suicide and the fact they will kill themselves provides evidence to the suicidal youth that suicide is a legitimate option. Particularly if a family member has committed suicide, the depressed adolescent can easily acquire the belief that she too is destined for suicide. This is obviously mythical, but it is a real issue for the suicidal person who is not wholly rational.

Youth Who Talk or Write about Suicide Are at Risk

As a form of denial, adults and peers convince themselves that children writing or talking about suicide are only seeking attention or venting their feelings and thus will not kill themselves. This is patently false; in most cases, after a completed suicide, one can look back and see a wide variety of warning signs. Children who write or talk about suicide are indeed looking for attention, indicating that they need someone to take control of their lives until the crisis passes. As will be discussed later, every incident of a child talking or writing about suicide should be considered serious and responded to immediately. Some children claim they are just writing poetry, and if they are really smart they will quote famous poets who have also written about suicide. I believe that the probability that such a depressed child is a famous poet in the making versus a truly suicidal person is slim. In such a case, however, look for other signs that the child is depressed or suicidal. In most cases you will find there is supportive evidence that the child needs help.

Suicidal Youth Are Ambivalent About Death

Children and adolescents don't absolutely want to die, like an elderly person with a chronic illness, for example. Youth have not experienced life and have little basis on which to make the decision to take their own lives. In their ambivalence, situational variables such as those described in the above section on precipitating events become very important even though they may seem trivial to the nonsuicidal individual. Thus, noticing these situational variables is key to early identification and treatment of a suicidal child or adolescent.

There Is No One Type of Person at Risk for Suicide

Indicators of suicide do not include variables such as ethnicity or wealth. All kinds of people commit suicide, and one should not rule out suicide as an option for a depressed individual just because he is wealthy or appears to "have it all."

Talking about Suicide Does Not Cause Suicide

The most important myth to be debunked is the belief that talking about suicide will increase the chance a person will commit suicide. The most important thing to do when it is suspected that a person is suicidal is to talk to the person about it. Also, there is no increased risk of suicide for teaching adolescents about coping with suicidal feelings or how to help suicidal peers. Some researchers have shown that schoolwide programs do not significantly reduce the frequency of suicide, but no research shows that educational programs made suicide more frequent. Some researchers, however, feel it is not good to teach children younger than ten or eleven about suicide prevention. This should be taken into consideration when planning a schoolwide education program with younger children. Information can be obtained from the American Association of Suicidology (4201 Connecticut Ave., NW, Suite 310, Washington, DC 20008, phone: [202] 237-2280, fax: [202] 237-2282) or the American Foundation for Suicide Prevention (120 Wall St., 22nd Floor, New York, NY 10005, toll-free: 1-888-333-AFSP, phone: [212] 363-3500, fax: [212] 363-6237) related to this topic. The bottom line, however, is that for a person who is suicidal, regardless of her age, talking about suicide will not make it worse; rather, it is the best course of action.

Helping a Suicidal Youth

In most cases of suicidal ideation or suicide attempts, it is best to involve a professional clinician to determine how lethal the person is and to determine a course of treatment. What does a parent or peer who is not a professional do when she discovers someone is suicidal? The following describes five relatively universal steps a layperson can use to respond to a suicidal person, including children and adolescents. In each step, do's and don'ts are listed to summarize the information. The following is a graphic representation of these five steps.

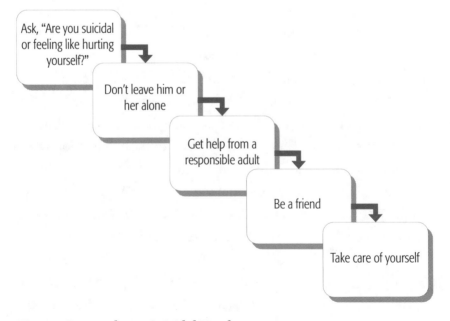

Ask, "Are you suicidal or feeling like hurting yourself?"

Don't leave him or her alone

Get help from a responsible adult

Be a friend

Take care of yourself

How to Respond to a Suicidal Youth

Ask, "Are You Suicidal?"

As discussed earlier, asking a person if he is suicidal or wants to die will not cause him to do so. If the person is not suicidal and you ask, he will not subsequently become suicidal. What this step will do is help verify your suspicions. If the suicidal person has shown several signs of suicidal intentions and denies being suicidal, you should continue through these steps.

Do's
- Talk openly about suicide
- Act quickly to help the person
- Clarify the permanence of death
- Remain calm

Don'ts
- Be shocked
- Argue against suicide

Don't Leave Him or Her Alone

There are several situations in which you may think that you should leave the person alone. A highly manipulative adolescent could talk you into leaving him alone long enough to complete suicide. Do not leave the person alone with the means to commit suicide. There are too many stories of people left alone with a gun or a bottle of pills when someone had just been available to help. Another predicament is when you have followed a person to a secluded place, such as to a park or into a desert or forest. This can be a scary situation, but if at all possible, get the person to accompany you to somewhere safe rather than going for help. Depending on the situation, there may be more or fewer options. For example, in the case of a parent with a younger child, you may physically take the child to a hospital; however, if you are a peer helping a highly agitated suicidal adolescent, there may be no other option but to go get help.

Do's
- Stay with the person
- Keep them talking
- Keep them safe

Don'ts
- Leave them alone
- Give them access to a weapon
- Give them access to any method of suicide

Get Help from a Responsible Adult or Clinician

For peers helping peers, it is a good idea for the peer and the suicidal adolescent to go to the nearest responsible adult and get help. This may be more challenging than it sounds; the suicidal teen may not trust adults she knows or may prefer to just talk with similar-aged peers. Calling a suicide or crisis hotline is a good alternative in this situation. In any case, find a trusted adult or clinician to contact as soon as possible. Parents can take the child to an emergency room, to a clinician's private office, or to a psychiatric hospital for suicide triage.

Do's
- Call their parents, a counselor, or a teacher
- Call suicide or crisis hotline numbers

Don'ts

- Promise secrecy
- Think you solved his problem by talking with him and then not get help

Be a Friend

When trying to maintain conversation and convince the suicidal person to get help, one of the best ways to talk to him is in a relaxed and friendly way. Showing fear or agitation will not make things better. Rather, remain calm and know that there are lots of options for assistance. Encourage the person to explore alternatives, including getting help from a responsible adult or clinician.

Do's

- Listen
- Show that you care
- Be positive
- Emphasize alternatives
- Follow-up later

Don'ts

- Minimize the problem
- Encourage guilt
- Give up hope

Take Care of Yourself

Dealing with a suicidal person, whether it be a peer or your child, is extremely stressful. Those of us in the business of crisis intervention often talk to our colleagues to debrief and diffuse the tension built up through dealing with a crisis. Debriefing is a good idea for the lay interventionist as well. Talk to a family member or friend and describe what happened. You will be amazed how helpful debriefing is. Associated with this step is not getting hurt or "going down" with the suicidal person. This is particularly relevant in situations with weapons or when someone attempts to jump from a high place. Know your limits and get professional help, such as calling 911 from a safe location in these situations.

Do's
- Know your limits
- Talk with someone afterward about the incident and your feelings

Don'ts
- Get overinvolved
- Try to physically take away a weapon
- Agree to a suicide pact

PHYSICAL AGGRESSION TOWARD PEOPLE AND OBJECTS

Hopefully, you have never been threatened or had your property destroyed by a depressed or manic child. This can happen, however, and it is important to know what to do. To understand how severe a situation can get with a depressed child or adolescent, consider the following vignette.

Rick was a twelve-year-old boy who lived with his mother. His parents had been divorced for several years, and there was a family history of depression on both the mother's and father's sides. He moved to a new school in the middle of the year. It did not take long for teachers to notice that Rick was highly irritable, self-depreciating, and agitated. He lashed out verbally toward peers and school personnel and did not like to be talked to or told what to do. When he was called to the counselor about his behavior, he sat calmly but was quite oppositional to the counselor's questions. On becoming frustrated, the child attacked the counselor by jumping out of his seat and slapping at the counselor's face. They both fell to the floor, and once she got her bearings the counselor called the school administrator and the police department. Rick was put in handcuffs. At this time it was discovered that Rick was diagnosed with major depression and obsessive-compulsive disorder, but the school was never notified. After Rick calmed down, his mother and the police officers decided it was best if Rick went home rather than get an evaluation from a clinician. Since Rick was already on medications and seeing a psychiatrist, it was felt he could wait until his next scheduled visit. That night when Rick and his mother were alone in the house, Rick wanted to use the phone to call a friend. His mother did not want him to use the phone at that time. A struggle for the phone ensued, resulting in it being pulled from the wall and thrown across the room. Rick started destroying the house and screaming at his mother. She ran from the house and called the police from a neighbor's home. When the police arrived they could hear Rick destroying the house and called for him to come out. On hearing the police officers, Rick quietly walked out of the house and was handcuffed and taken to a psychiatric hospital. Treatment continued in the hospital for several days, then Rick was transferred to a residential placement where he lived and went to school full-time for about nine months. After this treatment he was ready to return home and attend a private day school. Finally, he returned to the regular school and has adjusted quite well.

The vignette about Rick highlights a very severe coping style that put the mother, the child, and the house in jeopardy. The first thing to consider is that Rick clearly had an emotional problem and that his physical aggression was a result of an inability to cope and the need for someone to take control of his life. In contrast, as discussed in chapter 4, children with conduct disorder can be extremely violent and aggressive but must be treated in a very different way than Rick was. Conduct-disordered children who threaten the lives of their parents and destroy property are best served by the legal system. For Rick, however, his aggression was best treated in a mental health setting using the methods and theories described in this book. That is why the police did not arrest Rick nor were charges pressed against him. In some cases, an emotionally disturbed child may continue to exhibit aggression despite treatment. It then may be appropriate to press charges and utilize the legal system for the safety of the child and others. These situations are very severe and outside the scope of this book. In such circumstances, it is best to have substantial consultation from a trusted clinician.

The next thing to consider is that physical aggression toward people and objects does not have to be as severe as described in Rick's case. There are depressed and irritable children who may throw things or verbally lash out at people. These should all be considered significant and responded to immediately. If these acts of aggression are not dealt with right away, they will continue and worsen. It is very typical for someone who uses aggression as a coping mechanism to begin to use the aggression functionally—that is, the child or adolescent will use aggression or destruction of property to get what he wants even when not depressed.

Aggression and Depression

Aggression is a complicated behavior. There are different types of aggression, such as psychopathic aggression, compulsive aggression, and organic aggression. The specifics of these types of aggression are not directly relevant to this discussion, but suffice it to say that parceling out aggression related to depression versus aggression related to being a criminal requires an evaluation from an expert. The following is a hierarchical list of the spectrum of aggressive behavior:

1. *Verbal aggression*: insults, shouting angrily, and making threats of violence.
2. *Physical aggression against objects*: slamming doors, kicking objects, throwing objects down, or setting fires.
3. *Physical aggression toward self*: picking at one's skin until it bleeds, banging head against the wall or floor, self-mutilation (hitting, cutting, or biting one's own body), or attempting suicide.
4. *Physical aggression toward others*: threatening gestures, pushing, kicking, and physical attacks.

These types of aggression may occur either because of depression, or without depression. From this point on we are only concerned with aggression that occurs because of depression.

Understanding aggression is important to the treatment of depression because a large percentage of children and adolescents referred for psychiatric help were originally referred due to aggressive behavior. Many of the children referred for aggressive behavior have undiagnosed depression. These acts cause such concern that teachers and parents are compelled to seek help for the child. In fact, in schools there is the notion of the "bubble-up phenomenon." That is, the first children referred for help are the most aggressive and disruptive. Once the most disruptive are referred, then the next most disruptive students "bubble-up" and are referred. This is why so many children with only depression and withdrawal do not get help. They are often completely ignored and the last ones to be referred. After the referral, the clinician can determine the nature of the aggression and begin treatment.

There is biological and developmental evidence for the link between aggression and depression. The biological evidence has to do with the neurotransmitter serotonin discussed in chapter 3. A specific subtype of serotonin receptor has been implicated in symptoms of aggression, depression, and anxiety. Aggression is sometimes treated with a class of drugs called beta-blockers such as Inderal, which has an effect on these specific serotonin receptors. Recently, Buspar, which is a drug originally developed for the treatment of anxiety, has been found to affect these aggression- and depression-related serotonin receptors and has been used in the treatment of people with mixed depression and anxiety and for those with aggression and depression.

The developmental evidence for the association between depression and aggression has to do with the formation of secure attachments and the development of empathy. As discussed in chapter 3, the lack of a secure attachment leads to negative cognitions and the expectation of negative outcomes. Furthermore, secure attachments have been implicated in the ability to control arousal. Therefore, in addition to not being able to control emotions related to depression, a child without the benefit of attachment cannot control emotions related to aggression. Further, expecting negative outcomes and not feeling in control of one's life lead to an aggressive, controlling coping style. Empathy formation occurs after the attachment phase and is deeply related to the development of self-awareness that occurs during the second year of life. As discussed in chapter 3, children who do not develop adequate self-awareness tend to be self-focused and overly critical of themselves. Children focused on themselves do not develop the ability to identify with others' feelings and emotions and tend to be less prosocial and more aggressive.

The good news is that attentive parents can actually teach their children to be empathetic and prosocial rather than aggressive and antisocial. Dr. Nancy Eisenberg is a prominent researcher who has discovered the relationship between inductive reasoning and empathy formation. Inductive reasoning, or induction, consists of a parent pointing out the consequences of the child's behavior on other people. For example, if a child takes another child's toy the parent would say, "Now he feels bad" rather than scold the child. Induction has been shown to be effective with children as young as one year old and should be continued as the primary form of discipline throughout the developmental period. In older children, there has been shown to be a benefit to encouraging the child to make reparations for whatever transgression she committed after the parent makes an induction. Vague, emotionally charged statements such as "Stop that!" have been shown not to encourage prosocial behavior or empathetic understanding. Also, punitive discipline has been shown to negate the positive effects of induction.

What to Do

In the crisis situation, parents must resolve to refuse to accept aggression in any form. Arguing and bargaining with a child is counterproductive and will only result in greater displays of aggression later. When a parent argues or bargains with an aggressive child, whether related to depression or for manipulative purposes, that child will keep pushing the limits of the parents' tolerance. In therapy, it is amazing how much abuse parents will take and not even recognize that the aggressive behavior is abnormal until it is pointed out. If the child keeps pushing the limits in this way, the situation can become so bad that the child has to be removed from the home. The aggression will escalate up the hierarchy of types of aggression until family members and peers are threatened.

When verbal aggression first occurs, try to determine the function of the verbal outbursts. For example, is the child frustrated, irritable, feeling misunderstood, or seeking attention? If you do not feel comfortable doing this or are unable to identify the functions of the outbursts, then get help from a professional clinician. Getting help when the behavior first starts will save you incredible amounts of suffering later. There are also many books on parenting that can help sort out verbal aggression and its range of functions.

If the behavior has moved beyond verbal aggression to physical aggression toward objects and people, consider calling the police to help contain and calm the crisis situation while showing your child that the behavior will not be tolerated. Parents must be confident of their ability to take care of themselves and their property, or the child will continue to act out aggressively. In one extreme case an aggressive teenager organized some gang members to destroy his parents' house and taunt the parents at work. Granted, this is an extreme example, but it shows how out of control a situation can get if the parent is passive. Aggressive and depressed children can receive residential services from the local school district, and, if there is no way to control the child at home, it is important to take control of the child through the support of mental health services available from the school. If you cannot control the aggression, put the child in a place where somebody can and then get help for yourself so the aggressive cycle does not start again.

Proactively, aggression as well as depression can be prevented by adopting the parenting skills already discussed. These include encouraging your child to develop a secure attachment and fostering empathy using inductive reasoning rather than punitive discipline.

RUNAWAY

Running away from home is a definite sign of family problems and is often a coping mechanism of last resort for depressed children. Research has shown that youth run away because of poor parental monitoring, little warmth and support from the parents, and high levels of parental rejection. Also, many youth who run away report a history of physical and sexual abuse in the home. In abuse situations, the family is so disrupted that members will not even view the child's running away as a crisis situation. In more stable families, however, where running away is a coping mechanism for depression, it is often perceived as a definite crisis situation.

Of concern is not only that the child ran away, but that he may have committed suicide. A family with a child or teenager who runs away should involve the police department and allow the child to experience the logical consequences of his actions. Repeated running away is highly stressful on the family, is dangerous for the child, and should be considered a severe response to depression or some other emotional problem. In these cases, hospitalization or residential services through the school should be considered. Letting the child live on the streets just communicates further rejection and increases the child's risk of harm.

CHAPTER 7

WORKING WITH YOUR CHILD'S SCHOOL

Learning in school is the primary job for children and adolescents. As such, when a depressive or manic episode emerges, a disturbance of school functioning likely follows. School functioning can be disrupted in a variety of ways, including academic and social functioning. In severe cases, these disruptions can result in very distressing behavior patterns, including school violence.

Schools also represent a vast resource for children with depression and their families. There are people in schools that can provide support and guidance, such as your child's teachers or the school counselor. Every school has access to a school psychologist, and some schools provide group or individual counseling on an ongoing basis. There are federal laws designed to provide extra help and services to children with emotional problems that schools call disabilities. These laws are underutilized for the treatment of depression because parents rarely know that depression qualifies a child for services. These laws are the Americans with Disabilities Act and the Individuals with Disabilities Education Act. The basic premise of this chapter is that children benefit more from education when their parents are involved and well informed. Further, parents are important members of school teams and are entitled to participate at all levels of decision making.

The purpose of this chapter is to describe the types of problems children experience in schools, to explain the range of services and options available to children and their families, and finally, to describe how to facilitate cooperation and successful service implementation for your child in the school.

DEPRESSION AND SCHOOL FUNCTIONING

Academic Difficulties

Childhood depressive episodes can last for nine to twelve months, which is as long as the school year or more. During the time the child is depressed, there may be particular times of worsening or lifting of the depression. These different phases impact academic performance in different ways.

Over the full course of the depression, the child may not benefit from academic instruction as much as he should. Several of the symptoms of depression do not facilitate good concentration or attention in the classroom. For example, hypersomnia may lead the child to fall asleep in class. Diminished ability to concentrate may cause the child to miss important concepts as they are discussed or miss the directions for an assignment or homework. In older children, when suicidal ideations are prominent, this preoccupation with death can sometimes consume all of the adolescent's mental energy. For example, a middle school student may come to school dressed in all black and repeatedly write words about death on her notebook or papers. In these situations, the student rarely completes work and is often only willing to complete writing assignments about death or suicide.

Most academic instruction is cumulative, and missing significant portions of instruction or whole teaching units can have a serious impact on the rest of the student's academic career. If the child is hospitalized for a period of time due to a depressive episode, she will miss out on a substantial amount of school. In some psychiatric hospitals there are relatively good schools, but they rarely cover what the child would be learning if she were in her regular school. Homework can be picked up for the hospitalized child, but it is rarely completed because of the lack of instructional support and demands on the child's time due to the treatment while hospitalized.

The following are a range of behaviors that may be exhibited by a depressed child or adolescent that exacerbate academic difficulties.

- *Tardiness.* Younger children often come late to school because of arguing among family members or because they are reluctant to go to school. Older children are late because of hypersomnia, lethargy due to fatigue, or rebelliousness toward parents or siblings in the morning.
- *Absenteeism.* Chronic absenteeism can be a sign of abuse in younger children, which increases the chances of depression. Financial burdens may force a child to baby-sit while a parent goes to work. Older depressed children may not be able to get out of bed at all due to fatigue or being withdrawn. Others may be engaging in risk-taking behavior

during the day, using drugs or alcohol, or hiding from school and family members.

- *Ditching school.* Children may leave in the middle of school because they just cannot take the social or academic pressures. They may feel like escaping and withdrawing due to severe negative self-statements or negative interactions.
- *Failure to see the relevance of school.* Depressed children experience a diminished interest in normal activities, including school, and as a defense mechanism, often say they don't care about school. Also, they may feel worthless and not believe their efforts in school will get them anything in the future.
- *Inability to tolerate structure.* The concentration necessary for children to listen to the rules of activities, follow through on those rules, and persistently follow structure is relatively high compared with the concentration available to the depressed child. Children will resist the structure just to avoid the effort it requires to follow the rules.
- *Daydreaming.* The child may appear to be "gazing off into space" and is off task and not attending.
- *Manipulation of objects.* If the child is unable to concentrate on instruction, she may play with objects on the desk or in her notebook. A depressed child with a calculator in her notebook may frequently play with it rather than attend to instruction.
- *Low frustration tolerance.* Children with depression may not be able to work on tasks long enough to gain educational benefit because they become frustrated so quickly.

- *Social withdrawal.* Often children who want to be alone fail academic exercises requiring group effort such as science or working at academic stations.
- *Poor organization.* Depressed children may not put forth effort into organizing their materials, may frequently lose necessary items and assignments, and may waste a lot of time because they are unable to get organized.

Social Difficulties

A primary goal for a child in school is to develop social competencies such as making friends, acting properly in social situations, and developing empathy. One of the most common complaints I hear from depressed children is that they don't have any friends. This is particularly troubling because the lack of friendships is such a salient issue in schools. Peers know who the loner is and often will tease him. Depressed and lonely children magnify their isolation and often feel like everybody is watching them, thinking what losers they are. These feelings obviously lead to more withdrawal and depression.

A lack of friends not only makes the depression worse, it is most likely caused by the depression. In particular, important emotional responses often have not been developed, as described in chapter 3. Also, these children may be overly affected by common jokes or talk among peers due to overpersonalization; they feel like they are not part of the group. A depressed child may experience difficulties in any of the following important skills for developing and maintaining friendships:

- The child may not be able to start a friendship. He may be awkward when first meeting a peer, may not reciprocate conversation, or may not engage in basic reciprocal play.
- The child may not be able to keep friends. To maintain friendships a child must initiate contact, generate age-appropriate activities, and keep confidences.
- A depressed child may not be able to share with others and can at times be rude toward peers.
- Children who have not had many friends may become overly possessive. They may cling to friends or get too close to them (known as violating someone's personal space), which is quite off-putting to most children.
- A depressed and irritable child may initiate arguments or fights. When feeling down or irritable, the child may not be able to apologize to regain a friendship.

Another aspect of social development learned in part at school is social skills. There are different ways of conceptualizing social skills, but Drs. Frank Gresham and Stephen Elliott have developed the acronym CARES to aid in remembering the important social skills a child must learn. CARES stands for cooperation, assertion, responsibility, empathy, and self-control.

1. *Cooperation* includes sharing with others, helping peers and adults, and following rules.
2. *Assertion* includes initiating contact with others, such as asking for information or inviting a peer to play, and responding to pressure from peers. Assertion includes the ability to refuse peers, such as the famous "Just Say No" program.

3. *Responsibility* includes being able to communicate with adults appropriately, to care for one's property, and to follow through on commitments.

4. *Empathy* includes the ability to understand the feelings of others, including being able to view situations from another's perspective.

5. *Self-control* includes accepting feedback appropriately, using win-win problem solving rather than fighting, and inhibiting inappropriate statements.

When considering if a child has a social skills problem associated with her depression, or if the deficit is contributing substantially to maintaining the depression, one must consider whether the child is refusing to use the skill, or if the child does not possess the skill; that is, does the child have a social skills acquisition deficit (has not learned the skills), or does the child have a social skills performance deficit (does not use the skills he has learned)? The other issue to consider is if interfering problem behaviors are involved in the social skills deficit. Interfering problem behaviors emerge in the depressed child, particularly when there is irritability and/or the child is exhibiting aggressive behavior. When there are interfering problem behaviors, one must control the behavior as well as teach the social skills or reinforce their use.

An example of a child with severe depression with associated social problems is a nine-year-old boy who was placed in a supportive classroom for children with emotional problems. This boy was able to have only one friend at a time because he was extremely possessive of the friendship. He would not let the current friend play with other children and would interrupt class to be near his friend. The boy showed a number of social skills deficits, including problems with cooperation and self-control, which made his ability to have and maintain friends even more problematic. When this child was in eighth grade, he had his first girlfriend. This lasted about one week because, although he had overcome some of the possessive problems with male peers, he reverted back to this pattern with the girlfriend. She promptly broke up with him and clearly told him not to come around her. In counseling it did not take much for him to gain insight into this old behavior pattern, and he was taught to self-monitor his need to be possessive in his next effort at an amorous relationship.

MANDATORY SCHOOL SERVICES

Children with emotional problems can often find substantial support from school personnel. A good teacher who demonstrates caring and concern for a child while encouraging her to be independent can go a long way toward helping a depressed child. School counselors often provide group and individual counseling, and there are social workers to help families at risk. This may not be enough, however, or a particular school district may not believe it is their duty to provide a full range of services. There are two federal laws that were developed to protect children with disabilities, including depression.

The most widely referenced law is called the Education of All Handicapped Children Act, which was originally passed in 1975 (sometimes referred to as Public Law 94-142). This is the law that defines all of the rules for special education in schools. Now in its second revision, this law is now called the Individuals with Disabilities Education Act (IDEA). You may hear school personnel refer to this law simply as "IDEA." The second law that applies to children with disabilities, including depression, is Section 504 of the Rehabilitation Act of 1973. You may hear school personnel refer to this law as it applies to schools simply as "Section 504."

Special Education

Special education comprises the rules, procedural safeguards, and services defined by the Individuals with Disabilities Education Act (herein referred to as IDEA) and covers people with disabilities (including depression) in public and private education from birth to the end of the twenty-first year of age. For those without experience with it, the term *special education* may invoke images of out-of-the-way portable classrooms with ramps and little buses. You may want to ask your child what he knows about special education; you may be surprised how knowledgeable he is. Over the past decade there has been an inclusion movement in special education. This means that children with disabilities, to a much greater extent than before, are receiving educational services in regular classrooms. This has resulted in a substantial reduction in stigma for children receiving special education services. Further, children not receiving special education are much more understanding of and receptive toward those with disabilities.

Who Is Eligible for Special Education?
As I mentioned, children and young adults with disabilities are covered by special education services until the end of their twenty-first

year. IDEA is relatively clear about what disabilities are covered. The names of the disabilities included in IDEA are not exactly like the disabilities covered in the *Diagnostic and Statistical Manual of Mental Disorders, Fourth Edition (DSM-IV)*, the manual of diagnostic rules used by psychologists and psychiatrists, covered in chapter 2. In IDEA, the diagnostic categories were written by the U.S. Congress with consultation from psychologists, psychiatrists, speech pathologists, occupational therapists, and many others. So the diagnostic criteria written into the law are more like guidelines and, in some cases, are difficult to interpret. Probably the most clearly stated diagnostic criteria is that for specific learning disabilities, which will be described below. The diagnostic criteria for depression, on the other hand, are considerably more ambiguous than what is described in the *DSM-IV.* Also, the determination for eligibility for special education is not made by a single professional; rather, it is made by a committee called the multidisciplinary team that includes the child's parents. There are pros and cons to this method (ambiguous definitions and team decision making), but the bottom line is that it is incumbent on parents to be informed as to the problems their child faces in the school to be sure the proper diagnosis is given.

Preschool Children

First, we will discuss the disabilities under which preschool children are covered. A process called *child find* is indicated by the law that requires schools to conduct free screening to identify children who potentially have a disability that qualifies them for special education. While child find applies to all ages, you may hear of preschool-specific child find efforts called "preschool screenings." If you are interested in your child undergoing such screenings, simply contact the school district within which you live. Child find was instituted with several purposes in mind. First, schools should identify children with disabilities not identified by other clinicians, such as pediatricians. Some cognitive and emotional disabilities require testing that a physician does not have time for or does not regularly perform with children. Second, screening can determine if there are developmental problems about which parents may not know. For example, related to depression, a parent may not know that a child's extreme irritability is a treatable disorder and may only think it is his personality or temperament. Especially with depression, false information in some professional circles that depression does not exist in children may delay a child's treatment for months or years. Third, screening can determine if previously identified children are progressing. Often children are diagnosed with developmental problems at birth or soon after. These children are referred to medical settings, and interventions are instituted. For example, phenylketonuria (PKU) is a metabolic disorder identified at birth that requires the child be on a specific diet. If the child does not stay on the phenylalanine-restricted diet, cognitive delays and possible mental retardation will result. Such children should be evaluated under the child find process and if cognitive delays emerge, the child and family should receive services. Older preschoolers found to be depressed should also be evaluated under the child find process to make sure treatments are progressing. Finally, the child find evaluation information is supposed to help with school program planning and individualizing instruction for children. This is a noble goal with limited implementation at this time. If a child qualifies for special education as a preschooler, an Individualized Family Service Plan (IFSP) that describes the problems and treatments for the child and his family is implemented at the school.

The IFSP is similar to an Individualized Education Plan (IEP) that will be discussed later.

The following are the areas in which preschoolers qualify for special education:

- *Preschool moderate and severe delay* are general classifications for significant delays in physical development, cognitive development, communication development, social or emotional development, or adaptive development. Moderate delays are at or below the sixteenth percentile on a standardized assessment measure; this means the child is developing as slow as the slowest 16 percent of children the same age. Severe delays are below the second percentile; the child is developing as slow as or slower than the slowest 2 percent of children the same age. These two categories are broad because children during the preschool years are developing so rapidly and variably that it is difficult to make reliable diagnoses. The logic is that if general delays are seen early, the child should be given some help by the school, resulting in better outcomes. This is the category under which a depressed preschool child would be provided services.
- *Preschool speech/language delay* is an eligibility category generally diagnosed by a speech pathologist and includes problems with language acquisition, receptive language, and expressive language.

For preschoolers, the areas of qualification are quite vague. With respect to depression, the school clinician will make the diagnosis in much the same way as described in chapter 2 and will rely for the most part on the *DSM-IV* criteria. In addition to these methods, the school clinician must gather information about the family situation and home environment. Part of the rules regarding developing an IFSP is that the family be included in the plan. This is very good for children exhibiting behavior problems and depression. Although it may seem threatening to be questioned about your parenting style, family relationships, and home environment, with objective feedback from a professional who has extensive training and has examined hundreds of children can only help. Applying information that is offered in a nonthreatening manner is an excellent way to learn more about parenting and family systems that exacerbate emotional problems. (Chapter 3 discusses the developmental causes of depression, and chapter 8 provides substantial information about parenting a child with depression.)

Elementary and Secondary School Children

There are many more eligibility categories for children in kindergarten through twelfth grade. At this point during the developmental period, children's personalities are much more crystallized and their problems appear more distinct. Also, children in these grades have some history with their school and teachers, which helps in noticing subtle problems. I will describe all the qualification categories for completeness, but I will focus most attention on the category that covers childhood depression.

- *Mental retardation* includes children that have both significant deficits in intellectual functioning and deficits in adaptive functioning. Intelligence is assessed using a standardized intelligence test measuring verbal, spatial, memory, and nonverbal reasoning abilities. Adaptive functioning includes daily living skills such as toileting, eating, dressing, and cleaning oneself; social skills; communication; and navigating one's environment. There are three levels of mental retardation: mild, moderate, and severe. Depression can occur along with mental retardation, and its treatment is often complicated by the child's limited intellectual abilities.

- *Hearing, visual, and orthopedic impairment* are three areas of qualification covering basic sensory and motor systems. These types of impairments are often very obvious to others and can lead to feelings of worthlessness and alienation. It is important to proactively provide counseling if a child is not adjusting to her congenital or acquired physical disability.

- *Traumatic brain injury* is the classification for anyone who has sustained a head injury and suffered physical, cognitive, and/or emotional problems as a result after the postnatal period; that is, the problem is not congenital or related to birth trauma. Traumatic brain injury can result in childhood depression as well as other emotional problems, because personality is frequently affected by brain damage.

- *Autism* is a disorder affecting a child's social, language, and behavior development. Socially, autistic children are quite aloof from personal relationships. Language skills can range from nonexistent all the way to good language with poor language pragmatics and poor intonation. Children with autism often exhibit stereotypic behavior, such as flapping their hands in front of their faces or engaging in repetitive self-stimulation, such as spinning objects and then watching them spin over and over.

- *Other health impaired* is a category for physical disabilities not covered by other classifications. When you finish reading this list, you may note that the very popular diagnosis of attention-deficit/hyperactivity disorder (ADHD) is not included in the law. Children with ADHD have some combination of inattention, overactivity, and impulsivity and, if it is very severe, qualify for special education under the category of other health impaired. Attention-deficit/hyperactivity disorder is also a qualifying disorder under Section 504 (discussed later in this chapter).

- *Speech/language impairment* includes significant difficulties with language acquisition, receptive language, and expressive language. This includes children who stutter and have problems with language pragmatics.

- *Specific learning disabilities* are the most frequently identified handicapping condition in special education. There are seven areas of learning disabilities: basic reading, reading comprehension, mathematics calculation, mathematics reasoning, written expression, oral expression, and listening comprehension. As many as 50 percent of children with learning disabilities suffer from some type of emotional problem as well, including depression. Learning disabilities can be very demoralizing, as learning is the fundamental job of a school-aged child, and significant problems are very apparent to the child and his peers by the third grade.

- *Emotional disability* is the category in which depressed children qualify for special education. To qualify for special education as emotionally disabled, the child must exhibit one or more of the following characteristics over a long period of time and to a marked degree, adversely affecting educational performance:

- an inability to learn that cannot be explained by intellectual, sensory, or health factors including behavioral disorders such as intermittent explosive disorder;
- an inability to build or maintain satisfactory interpersonal relationships with peers and teachers;
- inappropriate types of behavior or feelings under normal circumstances, including schizophrenia;
- a tendency to develop physical symptoms or fears associated with personal or school problems, including different forms of anxiety;
- a general pervasive mood of unhappiness or depression, including negative affectivity or mixed anxiety and depressive disorder and bipolar disorder.

It may be obvious that depression can occur with practically all of the other disabilities under which a child may qualify for special education. The diagnosis and classification for depression are not made, however, unless the child is experiencing a significant depressive or manic episode. School clinicians make the diagnosis the same way as discussed in chapter 2. In addition, parents may have their children evaluated by a private clinician. If the private clinician writes a comprehensive report and makes the diagnosis as one of the types of depression, most schools will accept the report and subsequently qualify the child for special education as emotionally disabled.

What Is Provided by Special Education?

The special education law IDEA encompasses is a lot more than just what it means to qualify for special education. There are a variety of services and procedural safeguards guaranteed by qualifying. For example, once a child qualifies she may move to any other school district in the country and automatically qualify for services. Imagine if a child were receiving a high level of services, such as being educated in a residential setting, and then when the parents move the child has to start in a regular class until qualified again— the results could be devastating. This right to services is protected under IDEA.

Specifically, children in special education are entitled to the following rights:

- *Free and appropriate public education* regardless of severity or nature of the disability. That is, a child in a severe manic episode cannot be told she must stay at home until the episode is over. Education and treatment must be provided.
- *Nondiscriminatory assessment* means the child will be evaluated without bias in testing or personnel, and if the parents are not satisfied with the school's evaluation, they can get a private evaluation paid for by the school district.
- *An Individualized Education Plan* must be developed detailing the child's strengths and weaknesses and the goals to be achieved by the modified education.
- *Due process* is afforded to both the parents and the school if there is a disagreement. There is a set procedure resulting in a due process hearing with an unbiased hearing officer. This routine is designed to solve most disputes without litigation. An important concept to understand regarding due process is "stay put." What this means is that during any dispute the child stays put in the educational setting he was in when the

dispute began. Thus, if the child was placed in a residential setting and there was a dispute, the child stays in the residential placement. On the other hand, if the child is not in a restrictive enough setting and there is a dispute, then the child stays in the less restrictive setting. This can be a serious concern when the child is aggressive toward peers or adults. In these cases, a hearing officer may have to intervene and rule to change placement for the safety of others.

- *Privacy and confidentiality* are protected. Specifically, records regarding special education cannot be included in the general cumulative school file, and only certain members of the school have access to these records.

- *The least restrictive environment* is selected for meeting the goals of the Individualized Education Plan. This relates to current efforts to include more children with disabilities in the general education curriculum. Also, it prevents children from being significantly excluded from regular education by placement in special public or private schools without trying less restrictive or less exclusionary settings. The hierarchy of least restrictive environment goes from full regular education with consultation to residential treatment in which the child lives at the treatment facility where he receives educational services. Severely depressed individuals with a high risk of suicide may be educated in such a facility. In this case, the rights provided by IDEA, specifically a free and appropriate public education, are very relevant because the school district must pay for the educational services in these extremely expensive residential settings.

- *Access to related services* is provided by IDEA. Related services include family training, counseling, home visits, special instruction, speech services, audiology, occupational therapy, physical therapy, psychological services, medical services (only for diagnostic or evaluation purposes), social work services, vision services, assistive technology devices and assistive technology services, and transportation.

The Individualized Education Plan (IEP) is the centerpiece of a child's special education services. Once a child has been qualified for special education by the multidisciplinary team, the IEP is written and the least restrictive placement is decided on. The educational placement is determined by the needs of the child and the goals of the IEP. The IEP is reviewed by the child's teachers every six months and rewritten every year by the treatment team (called the IEP team), which includes the parents. During the annual development of a new IEP, the child's progress on goals is evaluated and again the determination of educational placement is made. Every three years the multidisciplinary team critically reviews the child's eligibility for special education. After this triennial review, the child may no longer qualify for special education, may be continued in special education under the same handicapping condition, or may qualify for special education under a different handicapping condition. If the child continues to qualify for special education, an IEP is developed and educational placement is again decided on. These current evaluation reports and current IEPs are what parents should take if they move to a new school district.

Individualized Education Plans
The IEP must contain information about who participated in its development, the types of related services to be provided, present levels of educational performance, annual goals and associated

short-term objectives, amount of participation in regular education, and the determination of least restrictive environment. Present levels of functioning is a summary of what is written in the evaluation report and of what the child has been doing in class related to the area of disability.

For children with depression, it is important to include in the IEP specifics about grading and discipline. With regard to grading, children with depression may experience a range of academic and social problems (described in the beginning of the chapter). Due to this and their involvement in special education, they should not fail a class or a grade because of their disability. Severe cases of depression lasting as long as twelve months can impact a whole school year, and modifications in grading should be provided. Some of the ways grading can be modified include giving credit for work completion, letter grades based on reduced assignments, letter grades based on a lower percentage of completed assignments, or the child may be graded under the same standards as children in regular education. If the child receives services in a special education classroom, the grades are typically already modified because the curriculum is different. What is often not recognized, however, is that the regular education classes the child takes should also be considered for modification.

Regarding discipline in the IEP, there are several considerations. The first consideration is whether the child will be disciplined under the regular discipline plan of the school. If the child does not break very many school rules, then it is generally okay to have him or her follow the regular discipline plan. If the child tends to get into substantial trouble, however, possibly resulting in suspension, the regular discipline plan cannot be used, and a modified plan as defined by IDEA must be implemented. More precisely, if discipline results in removal from the full range of educational services despite modifications that are provided by the school to correct the discipline problem, an alternative discipline plan must be initiated. In other words, if a child has a discipline problem associated with his depression, the IEP team will always need to consider modifying the discipline plan.

It is not uncommon for a child with depression to be disrespectful to a teacher secondary to irritability, be aggressive toward a peer, or refuse to work. If the standard school disciplinary actions include suspension and the child gets suspended too many times, IDEA has specific steps to remedy the problem. The idea here is that children with disabilities cannot be excluded from education by virtue of the behavior they exhibit due to the disability. When a behavior results in a suspension of more than ten days, it is considered a violation of a student's right to a free and appropriate public education. This may include out-of-school suspensions in which the student is asked to stay at home during the school day, in-school suspensions in which the student is not allowed to attend her regular schedule of classes but still attends school, or a combination of in-school and out-of-school suspensions.

The process mandated by IDEA to address these more serious behavior problems is called *functional behavioral assessment*, which requires the school team to determine the functions of the behavior problem for the child. In the case of depression, these problem behaviors are typically coping mechanisms. After analyzing the functions of the behavior the school team must develop a behavior intervention plan that will address the problem with a specific focus on the functions of the problem behavior. If after implementing the intervention plan the behavior continues, the functional behavioral assessment must be conducted again and a new intervention plan must be developed. In any case, if your child is chronically suspended from school and has an IEP, the school must determine a better intervention than suspension and stop suspending your child.

Should I Put My Child in Special Education?

This is indeed a personal decision for the family, and, in most cases, a school will not dispute a parent if he refuses a recommendation for special education. The school does have the right to due process if a parent refuses, however. This is important because I have seen several cases in which the child desperately needed help, and for whatever reason, the parent refused services. If your child's depression or bipolar disorder is severe enough to result in academic failure, social problems, and discipline problems, there are many advantages to getting help from special education. If the school raises the issue of special education, it is worthwhile to go to the planning meeting and hear what the school team has to say. But if the issue is brought up, chances are your child needs help.

There are several typical concerns about special education that I have heard many times. Stigmatizing the child is probably most frequent. The fact is that many schools provide special education during only part of the day, and most of the day the child is in regular classes. Because of this, children not in special education have gotten used to their peers getting pull-out services (taking a specific class in a special education classroom) or getting extra help in the regular classroom. Also, with the right to confidentiality, the special education status will not be transferred to colleges, employers, or the military.

Another concern is that teachers just want the child out of the classroom or just want someone else to deal with the child. This is what the procedural safeguards are all about. You as the parent have substantial rights and can prevent any categorical removal of your child from a classroom or educational placement. If changing classrooms is the best thing, then it should be done, but only after you have approved and are comfortable with such changes. A good way to ease your mind is to talk with someone in the school whom you respect and trust. This may be the principal or it may be the teacher your child had last year. Ask that individual about the personality of your child's current teacher or teachers. Ask about the history of special education referrals from the teachers. If you find that your child's teachers refer to special education only when appropriate, then you should feel more comfortable about the recommendation. If not, then get a second opinion.

Another concern has to do with the reversibility of a decision to place a child in special education. You have the right to remove a child from special education at any time. Again, the school has the right to due process, but if you are feeling something is drastically wrong, do not hesitate to follow your instincts. Special education is not designed to last for the child's entire school career unless it is absolutely necessary (as in most cases of mental retardation and autism). That is why there are frequent reviews of the IEP and qualifying disability. The goal is to implement effective interventions, resulting in the child being successful in all regular education.

Section 504

Section 504 of the 1973 Rehabilitation Act is a civil rights statute designed to prevent discrimination against individuals with disabilities and to assure that disabled students have educational opportunities and benefits equal to those provided to nondisabled students. The problem was that the Rehabilitation Act applied only to public institutions receiving federal funds; that is, only public schools were covered by the act. In 1990, a similar act was passed by Congress called the Americans with Disabilities Act (ADA). The purpose of the ADA was to prevent discrimination against individuals with disabilities, and it was modeled after the 1973 Rehabilitation Act. The ADA extended the protections of the Rehabilitation Act to private institutions, including private schools. Thus, any school, whether it be public or private, is subject to the ADA and Section 504. The protections for children are basically the same in both acts, so I will refer to the rights provided by these two acts as Section 504. This is typically how you will hear school personnel refer to the rights covered by these acts.

Section 504 Versus IDEA

There are several differences between Section 504 and IDEA, the special education law. An important difference is that school entities do not receive federal funds for children covered under Section 504, while they do receive funding for children covered under IDEA. This is not all that important to parents, but it is very important to schools. From the viewpoint of the school, it is better financially to qualify a child under IDEA than it is to cover the child under Section 504. This will be explained in more detail later, but the fact is that there are many financial undercurrents related to schools providing services to children with disabilities.

Section 504 is much broader in scope in terms of covered disabilities than IDEA. That is, more children qualify for Section 504 than do for IDEA, but all children who are covered by IDEA are also covered by Section 504. When a school qualifies a child with a handicapping condition under IDEA, it typically does not qualify the child under Section 504. This would represent a substantial redundancy in procedure.

Section 504 does not have the range of procedural safeguards that are written into IDEA. As discussed previously, in IDEA multidisciplinary evaluations must be conducted every three years, and the Individualized Education Plan must be rewritten every year. In Section 504, the only similar requirement is to conduct a reevaluation before a significant change in services. Another difference is that IDEA requires modifications of the educational program to provide the child with a free and appropriate public education (FAPE), a legally defined concept for the full range of education at the public expense. In Section 504, only reasonable modifications and accommodations must be made. Thus, under Section 504 your child can be suspended for more than the restricted ten days in IDEA. Also, schools are not required to conduct a functional behavioral analysis or behavior intervention plan as mandated by IDEA. Another difference has to do with confidentiality. The Section 504 records can be included in a child's cumulative school record, and Section 504 provides much less protection regarding confidentiality than does IDEA.

There are many other differences between Section 504 and IDEA, but they are too technical for the scope of this book. What should be garnered from the discussion of these differences is that:

- Children who do not qualify for IDEA may qualify for Section 504 protections and educational modifications and accommodations.
- It is redundant to qualify a child under Section 504 if the child already qualifies for IDEA because there is redundancy

in procedure, there are more rights provided by IDEA, and there is no additional funding available to the school district for Section 504 qualification.

Depression and Section 504

You might ask what the relevance of Section 504 for a depressed child is, given that depression is covered under IDEA. The first has to do with the length of the depressive or manic episode. A child does not have to have a history of academic failure or social problems as defined by the school to have a depressive episode; that is, the depressive or manic episode can come out of nowhere in the eyes of the school. The school then may say the child does not qualify for IDEA because the disability has not manifested for "a long period of time and to a marked degree, which adversely affects educational performance." The school personnel may say that they should just wait until the depressive phase passes to determine if there really is a long-term disability. Further, in cases of bereavement, there may be disruption of school functioning, but of an acute nature so that a school could say it does not qualify the child. In these cases, services still can be provided under Section 504.

It is unreasonable to let a child fail and deny the necessary support just because the depression is acute and is a child's first episode. Such a situation really represents early identification, and a legal case probably could be made that the child would qualify for IDEA. This is not convenient for most parents, however, and denies the child services during the period of litigation. So while waiting to meet the standard of "a long time", the child will qualify for modifications and accommodations under Section 504.

Another situation in which Section 504 is useful for depressed children is when the child has a history of depression but has met the exit criteria for IDEA. When a child meets the goals of his or her IEP for a significant period of time, there is no reason to continue the services. One could argue that the IEP is working and that this is why the child is meeting his goals. But over the course of a child's disability, school personnel should strive for the least restrictive environment. This means that as the child continues to succeed, services should be slowly phased out. As services are phased out and the child continues to succeed, a case can be made to discontinue IDEA services. When a child is phased out of services there are situations where the child may not be monitored or the history of potential problems will not follow the child through her academic career. This includes transitions from elementary school to middle school or from middle school to high school. In these cases, it may be wise to develop a Section 504 plan to protect the child in case of a relapse. A big difference between Section 504 and IDEA is that the documentation may be included in the child's cumulative school record and is not subject to the level of confidentiality provided by IDEA. This is good for protecting the child during school transitions, but it may be a concern to those wishing to maintain confidentiality. This is an individual decision and must be weighed carefully.

Initiating School Services

Now that you have an introduction to how depression impacts school functioning and the major laws covering children with depression, we must consider the steps necessary to initiate these services. Parents have the right to contact their child's school and request that the child be considered for special education or Section 504 services. In the last two sections of this chapter I will describe the full range of special education services with the under-standing that Section 504 services may be indicated rather that IDEA services. The process for beginning services is basically the same under both laws.

The philosophy of the school regarding special education should be something like this: If the child really needs significant changes to the educational program to benefit from instruction and cannot be helped effectively without these modifications, then the process of special education should be started. On the other hand, if less drastic modifications can help a child, then the process of labeling and qualifying a child for special education should be avoided. How does the school and the parent come to some agreement about this decision?

Prereferral Consultation

The first step is to conduct "prereferral consultation." A referral is the school terminology for initiating the procedural safeguards and rules of special education. So prereferral does not mean before school personnel or parents notice the need for services. It does, how-ever, mean that consultation and interventions should be tried and shown inadequate before the formal referral to special education is made. Consultation means that a professional in the school helps the teacher or the team of teachers generate ideas that will help the child benefit from education. School psychologists and school counselors frequently are involved in providing consultation. In addition, parents and other individuals not affiliated with the school such as private counselors, psychiatrists, or clergy can provide rec-ommendations to the teachers as well. Intervention means that someone in the school actually does something. It may be that the teacher provides the child with extra support, or it may be that the child gets counseling from the school counselor. Whatever the consultation or intervention, the school should do this before initiating a special education referral. The outcome of prereferral consultation is what is used to determine if a formal referral is necessary. If the consultation and intervention were effective—that is, the behavioral problems dissipated and the child performed better academically and socially—then there may be no need for special education. If consultation did not work, then there may be a need for special education.

Prereferral consultation is considered the best practice for school treatment teams. There are times, however, when parents or school team members do not want to conduct prereferral consultation. Unfortunately, in my experience, when a parent will not agree to prereferral consultation there is a conflict between the parent and the teachers, and the parent pressures the school to immediately make a formal referral for special education. This is rarely the best way to proceed because much valuable information is learned from prereferral consultation; often the problem can be corrected with just consultation and intervention. Also, if the results of the evaluation show that your child does not qualify for special education, the consultative process will then be initiated, but valuable time may be lost. On the other hand, if the school appears to be dragging its feet and not making the special education referral, it is appropriate to pressure the school. You will know this is happening because your child's grades are not improving, the school cannot explain what they are doing or how it is helping, and the prereferral consultation has gone on for a long time. Also, be aware that if it is getting close to the end of the year, some schools will claim they are doing prereferral consultation and drag it out to the end of the school year so that the formal referral does not have to be done until the following year. There should be a balance between the parent allowing the school to conduct some prereferral consultation and the school knowing when enough is enough and making a formal referral.

How do you know if the prereferral intervention is appropriate and effective? There are two aspects to consultation and intervention the school should be able to articulate to you to indicate it is truly conducting an effective prereferral intervention: treatment validity and treatment integrity. Treatment validity means that the intervention selected to be tried makes sense, given the problem the child exhibits. For example, if your child is exhibiting work refusal due to feelings of worthlessness associated with depression (he doesn't think he can do it so he doesn't try) and the school institutes an intervention such as not allowing him to go on field trips if he does not start his work, you should question the treatment validity. This is a punishment intervention that further demoralizes the child, isolates the child from peers, and probably would exacerbate the depression. The treatment does not make sense given the child's problem. A better intervention would be to modify the work so that it was absolutely within the child's range of ability and to encourage small steps toward completing assignments, resulting in reinforcing successes from academic tasks. This will result in increasing the child's academic self-concept and will give him or her something to be proud of, and not result in social alienation. Members of school teams should be able to articulate the purpose of their interventions in this way. If they do, you should have some confidence in the intervention and give them some time to implement it.

The second factor important to prereferral consultation decision making, treatment integrity, has to do with the actual implementation of the well-articulated and treatment-valid intervention. Treatment integrity means that the prescribed intervention was indeed implemented and implemented properly. Teachers often work with too many children and have difficulty finding the time to implement interventions. As a result, the recommended interventions may not be implemented or are implemented poorly. I have considerable empathy for this situation and I believe this problem should be corrected on a national level by supplying teachers with resources and manageable case loads; however, this is no excuse related to an individual child. When you are considering whether to continue prereferral intervention, you must consider if the people responsible for implementing the intervention are doing so and if they are implementing the intervention correctly. In the above example about modifying the child's work to increase academic successes, the teacher is now responsible for preparing the lessons for the class each day, as well as modifying the lesson for the individual child. This is time consuming, and if the teacher only does this modification one time per week, the child will not receive the expected benefit. The modification must be done every day to retain treatment integrity. When you are sitting with the school team making these decisions, the personnel should be able to articulate how they are implementing the interventions and demonstrate that they are doing it as much as indicated.

Treatment integrity is not limited to school personnel. Often during prereferral consultation, the parents are expected to do something such as check a daily or weekly homework contract. If the parent does not check this contract and follow through on helping the child complete his homework, then there is a breakdown in treatment integrity and the school should not be held solely responsible for the intervention failure.

When there is a breakdown in treatment validity or treatment integrity, one does not necessarily have to immediately initiate a formal special education referral. It is best to make sure the recommended interventions make sense for the child and that they are implemented correctly. After gently recommending changes to improve treatment validity and integrity, however, if those revised changes are without an associated improvement in the child's problem, you should request that a formal referral be made so that you have the protections of the special education procedural safeguards on your side.

Formal Referral

If the child's problem persists after prereferral consultation, then a formal referral for a special education evaluation should be made. The parent must sign a form, usually provided by the school district, giving permission for the special education process to start. The permission-to-evaluate form is not absolutely necessary. For example, if you have a hard time getting this form from the school district, you can simply write a letter detailing your concerns and requesting a special education evaluation. From the time of the signature, the school has sixty days to complete the evaluation and hold the meeting to review test results and determine eligibility for special education. That is really all there is to it.

If you do not agree with the findings of the evaluation team, you can write a note expressing your opposition and request an independent evaluation. As stated previously, the school will pay for an independent evaluation. This assessment may be done by a second unbiased evaluator employed by the school district or may be performed outside the district as deemed appropriate by the school. Some parents assume that they may pick their own independent evaluator that will be paid for by the school; this may not necessarily be the case. It is also not the case that the parent can go to several evaluators and then pick the report with which they mostly agree. In other words, you cannot "shop" for the diagnosis; this does not serve the best interest of the child. If there is need for an independent evaluation or due process hearing, you may want to contact the person in charge of special education. This person may have different titles such as special education director or pupil personnel director. Whatever the title, the buck stops somewhere. Simply call the district offices of the school district you live in and ask for the person in charge of special education. This also goes for children attending private schools whether or not within your school district; that is, you contact the school district within which you live.

The other time the special education referral process is initiated is when a child is repeatedly suspended from school and there is a suspected disability. This is part of the IDEA law, and if the school or parent thinks there is a disability accounting for repeated behavior problems, then the consideration for special education must be invoked. For example, if a child has some signs of depression and has become oppositional to teachers, resulting in suspensions, the parent can raise the issue that the child may have a learning or emotional problem. If at the time this issue is raised there have been a significant number of suspensions, the school must initiate the special education evaluation.

Typical School Modifications

There are a wide variety of interventions that a school team may perform for children with depression. If the child is placed in special education and an IEP is written, there may be a change in academic placement. Prior to these steps, however, some interventions should be tried. The following are some ideas of what to do for a child with depression in a school setting at the prereferral consultation stage of the referral process.

- For absences and tardiness, consider establishing a routine of completing success-oriented tasks or a special responsibility to be done first thing when the child starts each school day. Make a contract among the child, parents, and school with specific agreed-on times to wake up, what needs to be done in the morning, time to leave for school, and what will happen when the child gets to school.
- If the student does not participate in group activities or special events due to social withdrawal, consider allowing the student to choose which group he would like to work with or which of the special events he would like to attend. Giving control reduces the power struggle that may occur by forcing a child to do something. Also, encourage peers to ask the student to join a group or attend an event rather than being told to do so by the teacher.
- If the child excessively blames herself for situations she cannot control, consider discussing each situation with the child to show that the situation was not within her control. Also, have the student record her performance, good or bad, and show the natural patterns in her performance. Also, provide verbal, constructive criticism to all students in the class to help the child see that she is not the only one with difficulties.

- If the child is not motivated by rewards, most school teams are at a loss for what to do. Reinforcing or rewarding is a very common prereferral intervention as is punishment. Recent research, however, is showing a trend toward more skills training and self-management. This is a good thing, because when reinforcement does not work it is very easy to use consequences or punishment. Skills training is direct instruction and emphasizes practice on such areas as maintaining friends and developing social skills. Self-management is typically cognitive interventions that teach a person self-control and the ability to monitor what sets him off and how to prevent it. The most effective prereferral intervention for depressed children that is not motivated by reinforcers is to make the classroom instruction interesting and attractive to them. In cases of severe depression, even this may not work.
- For not accepting responsibility for behaviors or academic performance, encourage the child to ask for clarification on instructions and reduce emphasis on competition or comparison of completed work. By asking questions, she demonstrates taking responsibility, and by not comparing work, she has little or no reason to hide behind excuses for academic difficulties.
- If the student indicates that no one likes him, consider giving the student the responsibility to tutor a more challenged peer, or reinforce students in the classroom who make positive, supportive statements or gestures toward peers. Provide direct instruction to the student in small

steps on how to interact appropriately with peers so they will eventually like him.

- Sometimes depressed children will let their appearance go or not take care of personal hygiene due to feelings of lethargy. If the child does not take care of his personal appearance and hygiene, consider making a contract among parent, school, and child specifying expectations regarding personal appearance. Remind the student in a respectful manner about hygiene if it is not kept up and praise the child when it is. In either case, discuss hygiene issues in private.

- For children who tend not to smile or express happiness, consider asking the child to smile or ask why the child does not smile. Bringing this fact to the child's attention often causes the child to pay attention to it when he is not smiling. Consider including brief, humorous comics or videos in class, and remember to tell the child after class how nice it was to see her smile.

- For children who throw temper tantrums, consider not giving the child attention for the tantrum; if this does not work, have the child briefly removed from the classroom. In either case, the child must follow through on whatever started the tantrum. Do not argue, debate, or plead with a child having a temper tantrum; this will only make the next one worse. Be consistent and fair and after the tantrum, during a quiet time, explain very clearly that a tantrum will never get him what he wants. Reinforcing a tantrum by giving in is the worst thing a teacher can do.

- If the student's mood changes rapidly, consider maintaining a calm atmosphere in the classroom and teach the child to recognize when he feels a mood change is coming. Do not criticize the student, and encourage him to express feelings in a socially appropriate manner.
- If a child becomes overly upset when given constructive criticism, consider sandwiching criticism between praise. For example, a teacher might say, "I see you really tried on this task, but you need to make some changes here and here to improve it. I have really noticed you trying to increase your involvement, thank you." It also helps to be very clear on expectations and even give the student a check sheet itemizing the steps for the task, thus preventing the need for excessive redirection.
- Anger is a common problem for irritable and depressed children. In schools, consider teaching the child to identify what sets him off and to take proactive time-outs when he is feeling angry.

CHAPTER 8

PARENTING STRATEGIES TO REDUCE DEPRESSION

At this point, we have discussed a variety of topics related to childhood depression, including its nature, cause, and treatment. Whether or not a child is depressed, parents play a vital role in the care of their children. In their capacity as caregivers, parents play an important part in both the prevention and treatment of childhood depression. The purpose of this chapter is to offer strategies for reducing the risk or ameliorating the effect of childhood depression through effective parenting.

The diathesis-stress model of childhood depression has been echoed throughout this book. If you examine it closely, this model emphasizes the relationship among the biological makeup of the child, long-standing and immediate stress factors, and the resources the child has to cope with stress. The balance of this text offers strategies that parents may use to correct developmental causes of depression and to help children combat stressors. Topics will include signs that you may use to informally assess your child's symptoms of depression, ways that you may assist your child to reduce the risk for depression or to reduce depressive symptoms, and methods to help your child if he is receiving treatment for depression.

Early in this book several important topics about depression were discussed. Because they are important in helping you safeguard your child against depression, they will be reviewed.

The first topic has to do with stress-induced depression versus depression occurring as a result of relapse. Recall that some episodes of depression or mania may not have a clear and immediate environmental cause. Thus, in this case, the life circumstances of the child are normal and there do not appear to be any clear stressors in the child's life that may be seen to cause the depression. As one mother commented to me, "My daughter has no reason to be depressed." This mother struggled with the idea that she and her husband provided a positive home for their daughter and that their daughter had never experienced any of the risk factors associated with depression. Through a complete evaluation, however, including a social and developmental history that encompasses examining the child's family tree, the parents realized that several members of their respective families experienced depression or conditions associated with depression, such as alcoholism and eating disorders. Offering these parents the notion that their daughter may suffer from a biologically based form of depression not only relieved these caring and responsible parents of considerable guilt but also shifted the focus of therapy from only coping with stressful events in the life of the child to consideration of medication and training the child in cognitive and behavioral skills to reduce depressive symptoms. Rather than spending time modifying the environment, we worked together to find competent medical care, to monitor the effects of antidepressant medication, and to offer the girl alternative explanations for her depressive symptoms. Within weeks of beginning an SSRI and therapy, the girl experienced considerable reduction in the severity, frequency, and duration of the symptoms of depression.

In contrast to situations in which depression appears to have few stressful antecedents, there are many more cases in which there are observable stressors that initiate the cycle of depression. In these cases, life events and how they are dealt with by the child are the primary focus of attention. Although antidepressant medication has been effective in reducing the symptoms of this pattern of depression, its treatment calls for changing the environment by identifying and reducing current stressors and by teaching the child skills with which to deal with disturbing thoughts and future stressors. These are the points of attack that you and your child should know.

In many ways, parents are an extension of the therapist. For example, prior to seeking professional assistance, parents conduct informal assessments of their child by observing behavior and generating hypotheses about it. It would be highly unusual for a parent to arrive at the therapist's office with no preliminary ideas about the symptoms or their cause. Typically, a parent reports that she thinks her child has some problem and offers some explanation for the symptoms, such as the loss of a family member or a recent move. In this sense, the parent has conducted an informal assessment. I describe it as informal because the parent does not have the advantage of formal and systematic training in the assessment of children and depression. In spite of this disadvantage, the parent can contribute valuable information about the child's condition and its causes.

Parents may also be seen as an extension of the therapist by noticing their child's progress throughout the treatment. Typically, during treatment the therapist spends one or two hours a week with a child in the highly controlled and unnatural confines of an office. Because it is not the child's natural habitat, it is common for her to behave in a fashion that is out of character. Until the child relaxes with the therapist and begins to display depressive symptoms directly to the therapist, most of the therapist's information about the child is obtained through parent report and the direct report of the child. In contrast, a parent overtly observes the child at home and hears about his symptoms from other sources such as school personnel and neighborhood parents. Although therapists have been trained to know what to look for to assess whether treatment is working, they rely on parent involvement to assess progress. By knowing what to look for, parents are a tremendous resource for the ongoing treatment of their child.

A third way parents can function as an extension of the therapist is by modifying the child's environment to reduce the risk of relapse or to ameliorate its symptoms. Again, while the therapist has but one or two hours a week to work with a child, parents have many hours to shape, mold, and guide their child.

INFORMALLY ASSESSING YOUR CHILD'S LEVEL OF DEPRESSION

Before ever referring your child for professional assistance, you have engaged in some form of assessment of your child's depression. Before seeking outside help, you have raised questions to yourself or to others, such as "What's wrong with my child?" "Have I done something wrong as a parent?" and "What should I do?" Parents use their powers of observation to ask themselves, "Is there a real problem here?" This process of inquiry is a type of informal assessment.

But what do you look for when conducting your assessment? Often parents bring their children to therapists after trusting their feelings that something is wrong. Though parents are usually right in following their instincts that something is not right with their child, they can benefit from a more objective set of factors to consider to augment their gut feelings.

Aside from biology, the causes of depression include cognitive, behavioral, affective, developmental, and environmental factors. So how does a parent know what to look for? Keep in mind that the very people who formally assess your child—psychiatrists, psychologists, counselors, and social workers—were not born with the capacity to assess depression in children. They received training, just as you are obtaining by reading this text. What these professionals search for are the symptoms or manifestations of these various causes. By delineating the evidence of specific causes, such as family history of depression, we determine the nature and severity of the child's depression. Further, by looking closely at the symptoms, we are provided a guide to responding to and treating a child's unique form of depression.

Cognitive Signs of Depression

On first glance it may sound challenging to identify cognitive signs of our children's depression. Are we expected to read their thoughts?

In truth, cognitive signs of depression are among the easiest to detect. Our thoughts are reflected directly in our language.

Cognitive psychologists emphasize the interpretation of events. Albert Ellis looked for demandingness, awfulizing, and self-rating. Demandingness is the tendency to confuse thinking that we need or must have what we really only want to have; awfulizing is the tendency to think that life is awful when something does not work out the way we wanted; and self-rating is the exaggerated tendency to rate one's self as either good or bad for doing or not doing what "should" have been done. All three erroneous ways of thinking may be expressed in the language of the child, if the child is thinking this way. For example, a demanding child may say, "I can't live without going to the prom." The illogically awfulizing child may say, "I can never face my friends, because it is so terrible that I didn't get to go to the prom," and the self-rating child may say, "I am grotesque because no one asked me to the prom." As we know, there are millions of children who were not asked to the prom and grew up to be happy, well-adjusted adults. The key is to listen for the child's extreme and illogical interpretation of the event.

The cognitive psychologist Aaron Beck recommends that we listen for the specific types of errors in logic discussed in chapter 3. Examples of illogical thinking include:

- *Arbitrary inferences*: A child says she is a terrible student despite achieving As in her classes.
- *Selective abstractions*: A child says he hates school because he does not have a lot of friends.
- *Overgeneralization*: A child says nobody likes her because she did not get picked for the team first.

- *Magnification and minimization*: A child focuses on the two points he missed on a test instead of the 98 he earned.
- *Personalization*: A child thinks a friend did not call her back because the friend does not like her rather than her friend was grounded from using the phone.
- *All-or-nothing thinking*: A child thinks he is either good or bad at something but is unwilling to be just okay at it.

As you try to identify your child's illogical thinking, remember that, according to cognitive psychologists, we create our own emotional reality by interpreting the world around us in positive or negative ways. Donald Meichenbaum challenges us to stop thinking in negative ways by creating new and positive interpretations of life events. Later, we will look at cognitive approaches you can use at home to assist your depressed child.

Behavioral Signs of Depression

It should come as no surprise to you that behavioral psychologists look at overt behavior as the primary sign of depression. But what specifically? Well, certainly suicide attempts qualify, but there are earlier and less dramatic signs of childhood depression. In addition to the cluster of symptoms that defines depression according to the *DSM-IV* (sleep disturbance, changes in appetites, crying), behaviorists look at the antecedents (triggers), the consequences (payoffs) for the behavior, and the degree to which the child tries to get needs met or simply gives up, such as with learned helplessness.

If you examine your child's behavior closely, you may notice that the symptoms are directly related to specific settings; for example, going to the home of a particular friend or relative. Perhaps the symptoms are seen after your child returns from school. If you were practicing behavioral psychology, you would take a closer look at the elements of the setting that trigger the depressive symptoms. Having found these elements, it becomes an easy leap to modify the environment in a fashion that reduces the symptoms.

A child's social skills should be examined to determine if he is able to obtain reinforcement from the social environment. Does she violate others' personal space? Does he cooperate with his peers? Does she know how to keep a conversation going? Does he dress appropriately? These are just some of the questions you could ask when assessing your child's social skills. Refers to the CARES model discussed in chapter 7 for more ideas.

Behavioral psychologists who believe that the child has learned from experience to be helpless pay close attention to how often the child initiates activities with others and what kind of response (acceptance or rejection) occurs from them. For example, if the child's depression is due to failed attempts to get others to play, the child's world can be modified to increase the likelihood of other children reciprocating attention.

Finally, social learning theorists, another group of behavioral psychologists, might look at the role models available to the child. Often, children model or copy the behavior of their parents. If one of the parents has a history of depression, it may be that the child has learned to cope with stress by invoking the symptoms of depression. For example, imagine the child who observes a parent who goes to bed early when he or she has had a bad day. It would not surprise the social learning theorist if the child engaged in the same depressionlike behavior when under stress. If this were the case, the psychologist may want to consider working with the child and the parent to teach both of them more effective ways to deal with stress.

Affective Signs of Depression

Some would say that the primary sign of depression is affect or emotion. So what does a parent look for? Depressed children may display several different affective symptoms. They are sad, they get upset easily, and they have little tolerance for minor setbacks. Depressed children are often irritable children. It is no wonder that a common comment children and adolescents make when they are experiencing initial symptom relief is, "The things that used to bother me just don't upset me as much anymore."

Depressed children are often emotionally labile, meaning their mood changes from one state to another, without sufficient cause. For example, one moment they may be playing happily and the next they are angry or in tears. Often, they do not know the reason they are upset. Sometimes they explain why they became upset, but the reason does not appear sufficient to warrant the degree of agitation. The child is literally out of control of his emotions, quickly becoming angry or sad without any apparent trigger. This is frustrating for the child as well as the parent trying to identify what has set the child off. Often, the search for the immediate cause of the upset is fruitless.

Another sign is withdrawal. The withdrawn child pulls away from others, not wanting to leave the house or his room. Withdrawal may be an attempt to regulate emotions, to pull in to avoid engaging in a world the child feels is intolerable. Typically, the child does not make a conscious decision to withdraw from others. Instead, she seeks the comfort of her room or home, "cocooning" away from others.

A more subtle, but profound, affective sign of depression is anhedonia, the inability to derive pleasure from events that once were found pleasurable. Perhaps it is easier to draw from your own experience. If you have ever experienced some degree of depression, you may recall that the things you typically enjoyed did not appeal to you. For example, if you enjoyed going to movies with friends, you may have taken a rain check on a trip to the show. A common scenario is a parent coming to the therapist's office to report that her son just doesn't enjoy the forms of fun he may have before. For example, the parent may report that her child no longer spends time talking on the telephone.

Signs of Developmental Problems

Four specific tasks of early development were identified in part through research on children of depressed mothers (see chapter 3). It was discovered that if these tasks were not negotiated successfully a child may develop depressive symptomatology. A parent may or may not be depressed; however, mild difficulties in achieving these four developmental tasks may contribute to a child's depression. For instance, stressors may challenge a parent's ability to consistently meet the child's needs throughout the early developmental period. And, while no one is perfect, parents who feel that they are contributing to the development of their child's depression should counter that thought with the fact that something can be done about it. The key is to notice what first might have caused the problem and try to instill the proper resolution by changing your behaviors, teaching the child better ways of coping, and expressing in overt ways caring and love for the child.

First, does the child exhibit significant problems regulating her emotions? Is she frequently out of control when playing alone or in social situations? These behaviors have been related to poor physiological regulation development that is secondary to the child consistently not getting her basic physiological needs met and an instability of the early environment.

Second, does the child express a limited range of emotions? Are the child's emotional expressions blunted or limited to the extremes? These symptoms have been related to poor differentiation of emotions and difficulty regulating arousal. During the developmental period, it is important for parents to express a normal range of emotions and to imitate the child's emotions when appropriate. By selectively giving attention and encouragement, the parent teaches the child appropriate emotional expression in terms of type and intensity. Children who have not developed these skills tend to blunt their emotional expressions or give up emotional control altogether because of difficulty in regulating their emotions.

Third, does the child show anxiety when you are away from him? Does he have difficulty developing relationships with peers? Does he worry about interpersonal situations or have difficulty forming opposite-sex relationships? A secure attachment is fundamental to developing comfortable and appropriate interpersonal functioning. A secure attachment helps children develop feelings of safety from environmental threats and confidence to explore their environment. This is achieved through the internalization of the parents as objects in the child's developing cognitive and emotional schema. If a secure attachment is not achieved during the first two years of life, the parents can still do a lot to help their child change his internalized representation of them.

Fourth, is the child overly critical of herself? Does she lack self-esteem? These symptoms may be related to an early internalization of negative self-evaluations from the parent. How the child thinks about and represents herself as an internalized object is, in part, formed through early modeling of parent self-attributions and expressions of confidence or lack thereof.

Signs of Environmental Stress

A major factor in the diathesis-stress model of childhood depression is the role of environmental causes of depression. In childhood depression we look for two sources of stress—that within the child's microsystem (the child's family) and that within the exosystem (the child's school, peer group, and community).

Preschool children have few exosystemic stressors, as they have not attended school, are dependent on their families, and are buffered from their community by their parents. In assessing the degree to which family stressors may have affected your child, consider long-term chronic conditions as well as more immediate events. Listen closely to your child. Look intensely at how your family is functioning. Chronic conditions may include ongoing conflicts between family members, alcoholism, chronic health concerns, depression in another family member, or insufficiently or oppressively structured households. Consider the degree to which your household may be perceived by your child as stressful, hostile, or unable to care for her needs. Also, look at the more immediate stresses in your family. Ask yourself if there have been any notable changes in your family recently. Has there been a relocation, change of schedule, or addition to the family? Has any member of the family achieved a change of status (graduation, health concerns), redistributing the attention available to the child? An honest and open accounting may identify several factors that contribute to your child's depressive symptoms. Such an honest accounting also may identify valuable points of change. Family systems theorists see the depressed child coming into therapy as a member of a collection of individuals. The depressed child may be identified as the patient, but other parts or the entire system may be impaired. In this conceptualization, the child is a catalyst for change for the entire family microsystem.

Although the family remains the primary system for a child, the exosystem becomes more and more important as he matures. Two major areas of concern for the child are school and peers. Again, listen closely to what your child reports about these two systems. Take inventory yourself by talking to school personnel and observing your child's friends firsthand. How is your child being treated, coping, and succeeding in these settings? Does your child have a condition, such as a learning disability, that interferes with success and results in a negative self-image at school? Is your child being ostracized by peers due to misreading important social cues? Consider these factors in your informal assessment of your child.

As you can see, childhood depression is not a unidimensional experience. Typically, it has multiple interacting causes. Recall that a valuable way to understand the onset or risk of depression is to weigh the various risk factors encountered by your child. Consider your child's biological predisposition, way of thinking about the world, degree of learned helplessness, affective state, and stressors. By doing so you can estimate the severity of depression and identify which of these factors are best addressed to gain symptom relief.

WAYS YOU MAY REDUCE YOUR CHILD'S DEPRESSION OR RISK FOR DEPRESSION

The systematic yet informal assessment you just completed provides a blueprint for how you may reduce your child's risk for becoming depressed or for alleviating depressive symptoms that may currently exist. Just as you were an extension of the therapist by assessing your child's degree and causes of depression, you can again see yourself as an extension of a therapist. In this case, you are engaging in preventive measures or direct measures to alleviate existing symptoms of depression. In the latter case, it is assumed that you will be working in conjunction with a professional therapist.

Parents play an extremely important role in the medical treatment of children. No medications can be given to your child without your informed consent. Implicit in the term *informed* is the notion that you are offered an explanation of how the medication works in terms that you understand. Your physician should take the time to tell you how much medication your child will need, how long it takes to begin seeing results, and how long your child will need to be on the medication. In addition to knowing how the medication works, you should understand its possible side effects and what will happen if it does not achieve the desired goal. It is important to take an educated and active role in monitoring the medications your child takes.

Another important reason for you to be educated about your child's medication is that you are in a much better position to evaluate whether your child is improving. Earlier, the different amounts of child contact between you and the counselor were highlighted. While you see your child daily, the therapist may see your child once or twice a week. This comparison is more exaggerated between you and the physician. Typically, medications are given and a follow-up meeting is scheduled a month to three months later. Clearly you are in a better position to evaluate the effects of the medication on the frequency, intensity, and duration of the symptoms.

A final reason you need to be active in monitoring your child's medication is to guarantee that your child is taking the medications as they have been prescribed. Children can be unreliable, and antidepressant medications must be taken as ordered. Imagine that you think your child is taking her antidepressant each morning. Unbeknownst to you, she is only taking it about 75 percent of the time. On the next visit to your physician, because she is still showing symptoms of depression, your physician will likely increase the dosage or change medications, when the initial medication and dosage may be correct. It is for reasons such as these that parents need to monitor closely the child's medication.

Educating Your Child About Wellness and Depression

Children learn about wellness and depression in several ways. They learn from the direct experience of trying new things and receiving the fruits of their own experience. They also learn from the direct instruction of important people around them such as parents, teachers, and friends. The media and other agents in their environments shape their knowledge about wellness and coping strategies as well.

An important parental task is teaching our children the skills necessary to succeed emotionally in the world. These skills are important whether or not your child is depressed. If your child is not depressed, this information may reduce the risk of depression. If your child is depressed, it may help reduce the symptoms of depression.

In either case, consider your child's developmental level. Offer information that is developmentally appropriate. Younger children do not have the intellectual capacity to comprehend complex psychological meanings. They operate on a cognitive level that Jean Piaget, a French developmental psychologist, referred to as concrete operations. Prior to puberty, their conceptualization of the world is simple and not particularly psychologically minded. With these children, information and explanations should be made simple. About the time of the onset of puberty, children go through a significant intellectual change. Piaget referred to this change in cognitive development as the stage of formal operations. At this point, the child is able to assimilate new information on the level of abstraction and complexity of an adult.

Also, consider the needs of your child. Offer information that is sensitive to what your child wants and feels she needs. Even though you may be right that your child needs the information, if your child does not want it, it will not be accepted. To support this notion, just consider your own life. Think of the times you have resisted and resented people who try to tell you what you need. An effective strategy is to ask your child if you may have her permission to offer some suggestions. To a certain extent, it is a matter of appeal. Which are you more accepting of: "You need to hear this" or "May I offer a suggestion?" For some, the difference is like feeling force-fed versus being offered something. Also, when considering the needs of your child, try to be objective about whether it is your need or your child's need. Children, particularly teenage children, are very sensitive to this distinction. Perhaps you might seek the second opinion of another person who knows your child, such as your spouse or a close friend. In any case, approach your child by offering help and support rather than through force. In working with at-risk or depressed children, you truly catch more with honey than with vinegar.

Cognitive Safeguards

As stated previously, how we feel is determined by how we think. People continuously seek to comprehend, evaluate, and appreciate their world. We constantly examine ourselves, others, and the rest of the world around us. It is essential to adjustment to achieve a sense of self-efficacy, or competence. The sense that we have a sufficient degree of mastery of the world around us leads to increased effort, greater success, and resilience. A sense of incompetence leads to decreased effort, failure, and a sense of helplessness. A central factor distinguishing children who have a sense of competence from those who do not is the degree of rational versus irrational thinking.

There are a number of approaches you may use to increase a child's competence and self-worth. First, thought-stopping, a technique attributed to Meichenbaum, is particularly effective with worrisome children. Thought-stopping addresses the problem of repeating the same negative thought over and over. This private action is also described as unproductive worry, where the individual tumbles the same negative thought over time and again. The habit becomes so strong that the child grows frustrated by its intrusiveness. Because the child thinks this thought hundreds or thousands of times more than she tells you, be sensitive to themes your child may verbalize occasionally and assume that you are hearing the tip of the iceberg. For example, if your daughter says she is too fat two or three times a week and is preoccupied with her physical image, you can bet she criticizes her looks hundreds of times a day. First of all, ask your daughter if she wants to talk about how she sees herself. If you are correct and she is critical of her body image, she will probably be happy to tell you how bad she looks, making her covert and private thoughts accessible to you. Although you may be tempted to tell her that her thinking is distorted, experience tells us that directly countering the thoughts will probably not be accepted initially. If you tell her she is wrong, she will discount your comment and hold fast to her distorted self-talk. If you appeal to how frustrated she becomes because she cannot get these thoughts out of her mind, you may find more success. This is an example of finding out what she needs, not what you think she needs. Once she agrees that these thoughts bother her, ask her if you may interrupt her when she says negative and self-critical things. If you can, invite her to make a game out of it. Talk to her, perhaps about herself, and when she makes a negative statement interrupt her and say, "Stop." Then explain to her that she was just self-critical. Typically, the child will try to deny the self-criticism because the self-talk is so habitual and is going on outside of awareness. After you repeatedly point out the distorted thinking in a pleasant, supportive way, your child will begin to be more aware of her own self-talk. Encourage your daughter to monitor herself. Once she catches her own negative self-talk, she will begin to correct herself, privately telling herself to "Stop."

In his book *The Optimistic Child,* Martin Seligman, Ph.D., recommends a very simple process for helping children develop a more optimistic mindset. His technique is similar to thought-stopping but is much more general. Seligman says that children need to turn negative perceptions into positive attitudes by challenging their own thinking. Basically, a child must first learn to recognize her negative, catastrophic, and self-blaming thoughts. Second, the child learns to dispute the negative thoughts as if a third person were doing the arguing. Seligman believes that children have a natural ability to dispute or argue with peers, teachers, and parents. What they need to do is use this often well-developed skill on themselves.

Depressed children also engage in a great many negative evaluations; that is, they focus on the shortcomings of situations in the face of positive aspects of the same object or situation. Depressed children see the glass as half empty, denying the fact that it is half full. An effective strategy for a parent is to model and encourage positive relabeling. If challenged to do so, an individual can find something positive to say about virtually any situation. Although this sounds a bit Pollyannaish, the truth is as our thinking goes, so go our feelings and our behavior. Don't expect a child to see only positive. Well-adjusted adults often see the negative in things. The issue is the relative mix of negative appraisals to positive ones.

There are several ways to increase the frequency of positive appraisals. When out with your child, ask him to tell you what he likes about something. For example, when you are in a mall, ask your child, "What is your favorite reason for coming to the mall?" In effect, you have pressed your child to make a positive statement.

If you ask, "Do you like the mall?" you are likely to get a yes or no answer. Try to avoid these types of questions, as you will likely get short answers and find yourself playing "twenty questions" soon.

Another way to increase a child's positive statements is to ask her to tell one good thing and one thing that could have been better about an event. For example, around the dinner table, initiate conversation about what went well today and what could have been better. Although this approach may appear to encourage negative talk, it contains the negativity by framing the question as "What could have been better?" and it actively solicits a positive verbalization.

Depressed children and adults engage in catastrophizing, the tendency to quickly make an extreme and immediate leap from a small setback to a catastrophe. A simple example would be a child thinking that she will be sent to the principal and expelled because she is tardy one day. Another is a child who thinks that because his friend is moving he will never have another friend. For children who catas-trophize, the goal is to interrupt this rush to judgment and have them reappraise the situation. If it helps, you may look at it as an exercise in probabilities, crisis management, and reframing. For example, realistically, what is the probability that your child will be expelled for coming to school late? Unless you have the most oppressive school board imaginable, it isn't going to happen. Regarding the crisis management portion, how will your child deal with the embarrassment of walking into class late? You simply coach your child on how to quietly show the teacher the note you have written, sit down, and open a book. In the second example, that of your child's friend moving away, if the move is a local one, challenge the logic of never seeing the friend again and offer planned visits. Also, suggest telephone visits. Use reframing; suggest that your child now has a friend in another city and visits could be an adventure. The skill is teaching your child to make lemonade out of lemons by leading her thinking, coaching, and modeling positive thinking yourself.

Affective Safeguards

If there is a family history of depression, there are things you can do to protect your newborn. As discussed earlier, emotions play an important role in human functioning. They serve as a means of expression, letting others around the individual know he is experiencing distress and conveying the sense that immediate needs are not being met. A hallmark of youth is the limited ability to regulate emotions. Early on, expressions of emotions serve the infant child. The first form of communication is the infant's cry for food and comfort. Throughout life, emotions and their expression serve to let others know our needs. As parents, it is important to attend to and respond to the messages our children try to convey through affective expression and to strike a balance between overindulging the expressive child and failing to respond to appropriate communications of distress. If we assume that emotional expressions are forms of communication, being relatively responsive to them allows the child to transmit needs and have them met. This reciprocity helps the young child learn how to regulate his emotions.

Parents can also assist their children by teaching them through action the range of affective responses. Oftentimes, children are confronted by unfamiliar emotions because their parents have not displayed them in front of the child. Appropriate expressions of emotions allow the child to recognize and utilize these expressions without fear, doubt, or shame. In addition to the direct expression of emotions, parents can assist their children by offering them a range of acceptable emotional expressions. Disturbed children are often found at the extremes emotionally. They may be inappropriately expressive or unable to express themselves out of fear of the effect of their expressions of emotion. Parents who display varying intensities of emotions teach the child that each emotion has a full range of intensity and that they can be responded to in a healthy way.

Some of the more severe affective symptoms such as withdrawal, anhedonia, and emotional lability may be secondary to negative cognitions. So, to help a child be more social and less withdrawn and to feel that he deserves success and happiness, a parent could focus on the cognitive causes of these symptoms. Medication treatment also may be indicated in more severe situations.

One method I use in therapy is called *tagging*. The idea is to say or put what the person is feeling into words. Children who are wrapped up in their emotional problems often lose sight of what is happening to them. Putting a tag on what is happening to them makes it easier to talk about it. It then becomes more of a thing, or stage, rather than an overriding, debilitating feeling. For example, you might say, "You look sad today." There may be no response at first, but after saying it a few different times in a nonobtrusive way, a child will begin to respond. Another benefit is that it helps children symbolize their feelings through language. They actually begin to understand themselves better through knowing what is happening to them in plain English.

Behavioral Safeguards

The critical elements of the behavioral understanding of childhood depression include learning through rewards, consequences, and modeling behavior. Another important element is learned helplessness, the sense that the child is out of control of rewards and thus quits trying to obtain them. There are several lessons for parents to learn from the behavioral perspective.

One problem children with depression have is not being able to identify or enjoy the reinforcements of their efforts. Indeed, with the symptom of anhedonia, they may not even actively seek reinforcement or pleasure. A parent can directly intervene by helping the child identify and experience pleasure. For example, a parent may discuss with the child the appropriate feeling of happiness and how he might enjoy a feeling of success. Sometimes children will experience a success, but their enjoyment of it is only fleeting. Teaching this to older children can be challenging. One thing I frequently tell parents is that they should stick to their efforts at helping their teenager find enjoyment. The classic sullen teen is very persuasive at not wanting to do something. She may say that her parents are acting corny or treating her in an immature manner. The depressed adolescent typically does not feel motivated. She may feel that she does not deserve happiness, make up excuses, and avoid situations. Through perseverance, teenagers can learn to enjoy physical contact and verbal expressions of love. Although the child initially may not want the contact, they are inevitably reinforced and can feel loved when contact is given. The bottom line with this is that parents must make these efforts routine. Through practice and repetition, these activities, actions, and words will seem less corny and more normal.

That addresses the reinforcements; I will now briefly discuss the antecedents in behaviorism. Your child can address antecedents to bad feelings once identified in two ways: avoid them or get prepared to deal with them. Neither response is inherently good or bad, and balance is the best approach. There is nothing wrong with avoiding some situations. It is only when many situations are avoided to the point of withdrawal that a problem emerges. Think of avoidance as an easy, first-line stress reducer. Once a child feels better about herself and gains more confidence, she will avoid fewer situations. In fact, she may forget she ever avoided them at all.

As for getting prepared to deal with depression-causing antecedents, the child must garner social supports and embrace a mindset that he can at least cope and possibly succeed. This is similar to the notion of stress inoculation developed by Meichenbaum. Basically, stress inoculation is the process of giving oneself self-instructions, that is, telling oneself what to do in certain situations. Through self-instructions, the child is more prepared to cope with a situation. For example, a baseball shortstop does not just stand in the field and wait for the ball to come his way. Rather, he gives himself instructions about what to do if the ball is hit to him, if the ball is relayed to him, or if the ball is hit to another team member and he must participate in the play. A ball player considers all these contingencies and knows what to do by directing himself. The same applies to the stressful situations of youth. A child can give herself instructions on what to do if she asks a boy to a school dance, for instance. She could say that she will be excited if he accepts or she will be gracious if he rejects and hopes to see him at the dance anyway. The idea is that the child is prepared for the stress of the rejection and does not make the situation worse.

The self-control theory was developed by Lynn Rehm and is similar to stress inoculation in the sense that the child learns to give himself instructions but also includes the aspects of reinforcement described by the behavioral psychologists. Rehm provides a simple three-step process that is, at first, taught overtly to a child in the hope that the process becomes covert and self-initiated. The three steps are self-monitoring, self-instruction, and self-reinforcement.

By using Vygotsky's notion of the *zone of proximal development,* I will discuss how this process is internalized. Vygotsky believes that a parent teaches her child through a reciprocal process of questioning, leading, and answering. As the child becomes more sophisticated, the parent provides less information and encourages the child to come up with his own problem-solving steps. For example, using the self-control theory, a child becomes overwhelmed by homework, leading to feelings of worthlessness and depression. By identifying this antecedent process, the parent tells the child what he noticed and teaches the child to monitor herself for these feelings. The child learns to notice that she experiences stress when the assignment is given at school, contemplating it on the way home, and once she begins to work on the assignment at home. In this case, the parent could ask, "What can you do to make your homework less overwhelming?" The child may not be able to answer this, but the parent answers this rhetorical question and teaches the child how solve her own problems. The parent might say, "You know, if you broke down your work into little chunks, it may not be so overwhelming. Can you think of a way to break down your homework into smaller chunks?" By nudging the child along and, with practice, the child then internalizes this process of identifying the problem and generating her own answers. The next time a similar situation occurs, the parent may not answer the first rhetorical question but instead encourage the child to apply what she learned last time they discussed these problems. To conclude the self-control example, when the child finishes a small chunk of her homework, she should reinforce herself by calling a friend for fifteen minutes, having a snack, or playing a video game for a while. With each accomplishment (completed chunk of work) she learns to self-reinforce. It is hoped that the child will need to use external reinforcements less over time and begin to appreciate herself for her accomplishments.

Another important issue for a child to work on is social reinforcement. Direct instruction in social skills and practice can go a long way in helping a child make friends and get reinforced in social situations. If your child is older and resistant to a parent's input, then it may be the therapist's job to do this; but it can also benefit the parent to know what aspects of social skills her child may be lacking and be ready to discuss these aspects when he brings them up either directly or indirectly.

Clinicians who focus on the acquisition of behavior through observation have a great deal to offer parents. Prior to the 1950s, the prevailing view of human emotion was put forth by psychoanalytic psychologists such as Freud. In their view, emotions such as anger or sadness were pent up in a metaphoric labyrinth. If we experienced more emotions than we expressed, we accumulated emotions that went unexpressed. Bottling up these emotions was unhealthy and resulted in a crescendo or outburst of emotions, called a catharsis. Bottling up emotions was bad, while catharsis was good. Behavioral psychologists challenged this notion of pent-up emotions and catharsis. In a landmark behavioral experiment, children watched a video of an adult hitting a "Bobo doll." As the model hit the doll, he expressed how much fun it was to hit it. The children then were allowed to visit with the doll. The experiment demonstrated that the primary factor in expressing emotions was the influence of a role model, rather than the presence of bottled-up emotions. The point of this is to reinforce the importance of the parent to modeling for the child appropriate expression of emotions and strategies for dealing with stressors. Consider the quality of the role modeling you offer to your child. How do you cope with stressful situations? What do you say and do? What is your son or daughter learning by your example? To further illuminate this point, what did you learn from your parents about dealing with setbacks? How did your mother and father behave that safeguarded you from stress?

Seligman, also discussed in the section on Cognitive Safeguards, offers parents many practical ideas. Seligman introduced the concept of learned helplessness as an explanation for depression. He asserted that we become depressed when we no longer experience successes and thus give up trying to obtain them. For Seligman, a key to the resolution of childhood depression rests with the ability of parents to provide opportunities for children to succeed and to give them *choices*. By the time the child is recognized as depressed, she has reached the point where no matter what she does, she will not succeed. It is incumbent on parents to find age-appropriate opportunities for their child to be successful. If you consider the age of the child, you can estimate the various tasks he needs to master to feel successful. For example, a very young child needs to master toileting and putting away toys. A little later, the child needs to master being left at day care and, a bit later, going to school. These developmental tasks are but trace memories to us as adults, but when we were young they were very important developmental milestones. The challenge for parents is finding the balance, neither overprotecting our children by offering opportunities that are more appropriate for younger ones nor overestimating their abilities and expecting them to be responsible beyond their years. Overprotected children grow dependent on their parents because they are not expected to succeed at tasks that are within their ability. They often grow very frustrated at not being able to "stretch their wings." In contrast, children who are expected to face challenges beyond their true capabilities often complain of a profound sense of uncertainty and resent having to "grow up too soon." Parents need to be sensitive to the fit between what is being expected of their children and what the child feels ready to do. The best way to strike this balance is to ask your child if he feels prepared to take on specific challenges.

Working with Developmental Consequences

Remediation of the four developmental outcomes discussed is challenging since it may require substantial changes in the parent's own behavior. Taking risks in terms of changing your ways of interacting with your child should be commended and is necessary in order to address these issues.

Problems with emotional regulation may be treated with medications and therapy. Your role will be to acquire patience and help the child cope with a lack of emotional control. Researchers have made various claims that behavioral and cognitive-behavioral methods will help a child gain control. This may be the case for more cognitively based behavior problems, but, on a basic physiological level, structuring your child's environment and developing routines can help tremendously (your clinician can help you sort this out). You may have to work with your child's school to develop a similar routine and structure there. Correcting this problem will take time, and there are no easy answers other than medication and structure. As with all the issues discussed in this section, I believe that redefining the internalization of parent and mother by the child is the most rational, psychotherapeutic approach. This should be accomplished with help from a clinician who is familiar with object relations therapy.

Problems with emotional expression and difficulty expressing a full range of each emotion can be addressed through modeling, tagging, and encouragement. As discussed in the behavioral and cognitive sections of this chapter, you can teach your child the full range of emotions through modeling and encourage the increased, appropriate expression of these emotions through reinforcement and self-monitoring.

Issues with attachment and security are best addressed through object relations therapy and with the help of a counselor. Parents can be consistent and help their child set limits for himself through example. I often see parents become too lenient when their child is depressed. What the child really needs is a solid base from which to cope with her problems. By being consistent, by refusing to be manipulated by the child's complaints that she is being treated immaturely, and by not letting her miss a few days of school because of hypersomnia, you will show your child how to cope with the symptoms of depression. This notion of a solid base is important for all children and is also one of the most important skills you can learn to successfully navigate through adolescence. Set reasonable limits, stick to them, and be understanding but consistent—easier said than done, but necessary nonetheless.

Problems with self-esteem and self-criticism may seem intractable. Also, once you have applied the techniques described in the cognitive sections, you will see relapses that frustrate you. With consistent effort, making sure you demonstrate confidence and are modeling appropriate responses, over time your child will not have to work so hard at self-monitoring and disputing negative thoughts.

Safeguards Against Environmental Stressors

The final topic in the diathesis-stress conceptualization of depression is your role in ameliorating ongoing and immediate stressors at home and outside of home. It is not unusual for children who are referred for counseling to have significant problems within their families. Typically, depressed children have family histories of depression and other psychopathology, more than normal frequency of family crises, and fewer than normal family resources to cope with these stressors.

In cases of family stress, parents are challenged to look within themselves and correct family problems. Typically, children have very little control over the source of family problems; however, they are often the first to develop psychological distress because of their sense of powerlessness over the family's problems. Commonly, depressed children report that they spend much time worrying about problems such as whether their parents will stay together or divorce, whether domestic violence will ever end, and when their parents may stop drinking heavily. Clearly these are concerns that a child cannot resolve. One way to reduce a child's stress is to resolve these family issues.

Stress in the child's immediate community, including school, can be reduced through parental involvement. It is important that a child feel connected to her school community to prevent depression. One way children feel connected to their schools is to increase their involvement in school activities, such as clubs, newspapers, and sports. On the other hand, school itself may be the source of stress for a child. For example, the child may have difficulty with a particular teacher, peers, or academic areas. Most schools encourage and appreciate a close home–school partnership. Research has consistently shown that close work between parents and educators benefits children, parents, and teachers. If your child reports school difficulties, consider serving in the role of an advocate for your child by contacting school personnel directly.

CONCLUDING THOUGHTS

At this point, you have been exposed to a wide variety of ideas about childhood depression. As a parent, you should be commended not only for taking a proactive role in your child's treatment but also for taking a close look at yourself and your family. I am impressed by families who are willing to look inward in order to solve their children's problems. You should also recognize that new medical treatments are being developed every day. We are gaining a greater understanding of the psychosocial causes of depression, and, as a result, counseling treatments are more effective. There continues to be substantial hope for children with depression, and awareness and understanding is the place to start.

RESOURCES

Psychiatric Organizations

American Academy of Child and
Adolescent Psychiatry
3615 Wisconsin Avenue NW
Washington, DC 20016
(202) 966-7300
http://www.aacap.org/index.htm

American Psychiatric Association
1400 K Street, N.W.
Washington, DC 20005
(202) 682-6000
http://www.psych.org/

Psychological Organizations

American Association of
Suicidology
4201 Connecticut Avenue, N.W.
Suite 310
Washington, DC 20008
Voice: (202) 237-2280
http://www.cyberpsych.org/
ass/index.htm

American Psychological
Association
750 First Street, NE
Washington, DC 20002
(202) 336-5500
http://www.apa.org/

Depression Awareness,
Recognition, and Treatment
(D/ART)
5600 Fishers Lane
Rockville, MD 20857
1-800-421-4211
http://www.nimh.nih.gov/dart/
index.htm

National Depressive and
Manic-Depressive Association
730 North Franklin Street
Suite 501
Chicago, IL 60610-3526
(312) 642-0049
http://www.ndmda.org/

National Foundation for
Depressive Illness, Inc.
P.O. Box 2257
New York, NY 10116
1-800-239-1265
http://www.depression.org/

School-Related Psychological Service Organizations

The Federal Resource Center for
Special Education
1875 Connecticut Avenue NW
Suite 900
Washington, DC 20009
(202) 884-8215
http://www.dssc.org/frc/

National Association of School
Psychologists
4340 East West Highway
Suite 402
Bethesda, MD 20814-0275
(301) 657-0270
http://www.naspweb.org/

Books

Systematic Training for Effective Parenting
By: Gary McKay, Joyce McKay, Don Dinkmeyer
An eleven-book series published by American Guidance Service

The Caring Child
(The Developing Child Series)
By: Nancy Eisenberg
Published by Harvard University Press

Internet Resources

Psychiatry

Dr. Bob's Psychopharmacology Tips
http://uhs.bsd.uchicago.edu/dr-bob/tips/tips.html

Facts for Families
American Academy of Child and Adolescent Psychiatry
http://www.aacap.org/factsFam/

Psychology

American Counseling Association
http://www.counseling.org/

Dr. Ivan's Depression Central
http://www.psycom.net/ikg2.html

Online Psych, Inc.
http://www.onlinepsych.com/treat/mh.htm/

Albert Ellis Institute: Books and Resources
http://www.rebt.org/children.html

School-Related Psychological Services

The Federal Resource Center for
Special Education
http://www.dsc.org/frc/

National Association of School
Psychologists
http://www.naspweb.org/

School Psychology Resources online
http://www.bcpl.net/~sandyste/school_psych.html

COMMONLY USED ACRONYMS IN SPECIAL EDUCATION

ADD	Attention Deficit Disorder	ED	Emotionally Disturbed/ Emotionally Disabled/ Emotional Disability
ADA	Americans with Disabilities Act	EDP	Emotional Disability (separate facility private school)
ADHD	Attention-Deficit/ Hyperactivity Disorder		
AE	Age Equivalent	ESL	English as a Second Language
APE	Adaptive Physical Education	ESY	Extended School Year
BIP	Behavior Intervention Plan	FAPE	Free and Appropriate Public Education
CA	Chronological Age	FBA	Functional Behavior Analysis
C.F.R.	Code of Federal Regulation	FERPA	Family Education Rights and Privacy Act
CST	Child Study Team	GE	Grade Equivalent
DDD	Division of Developmental Disabilities	HI	Hearing Impaired
DHS	Department of Health Services	IDEA	Individuals with Disabilities Act

IEE	Independent Education Evaluation
IEP	Individualized Education Plan
IFSP	Individualized Family Service Plan
IHO	Impartial Hearing Officer
IQ	Intelligence Quotient
LD	Learning Disability/ Learning Disabled
LEA	Local Education Agency
LEP	Limited English Proficient
LRE	Least Restrictive Environment
MD	Multiply Disabled/ Multiple Disabilities
MET	Multidisciplinary Eligibility Team
MIMR	Mild Mental Retardation
MOMR	Moderate Mental Retardation
OHI	Other Health Impairment
OI	Orthopedic Impairment

OT	Occupational Therapy/Therapist
PL	Public Law
PMD	Preschool Moderate Delay
PSD	Preschool Severe Delay
PT	Physical Therapy/ Therapist
RTC	Residential Treatment Center
Section 504	Refers to Section 504 of the Rehabilitation Act of 1973
SLD	Specific Learning Disability
SLI	Speech/Language Impairment
SLP	Speech Language Pathologist
SMR	Severe Mental Retardation
SPED	Special Education
TAT	Teacher Assistance Team
TBI	Traumatic Brain Injury
VI	Visual Impairment

BIBLIOGRAPHY

Alexander, L. B., et al. "On what bases do patients choose their therapists?" *Journal of Psychotherapy Practice and Research* 2, no. 2 (1993): 135–46.

Alford, B. A., and A. T. Beck. *The Integrative Power of Cognitive Therapy.* New York: The Guilford Press, 1997.

Amanat, E., and C. Butler. "Oppressive behaviors in the families of depressed children." *Family Therapy* 11, no. 1 (1984): 65–77.

Ambrose, B., and W. S. Rholes. "Automatic cognitions and the symptoms of depression and anxiety in children and adolescents: An examination of the content-specificity hypothesis." *Cognitive Therapy & Research* 17, no. 2 (1993): 153–71.

———. "Automatic cognitions and the symptoms of depression and anxiety: An examination of the content specificity hypothesis." *Cognitive Therapy & Research* 17, no. 3 (1993): 289–308.

American Association of Child and Adolescent Psychiatry. "Practice parameters for the assessment and treatment of children and adolescents with bipolar disorder." *Journal of the American Academy of Child and Adolescent Psychiatry* 36, no. 10 (1997): 157S–176S.

American Psychiatric Association. *Diagnostic and Statistical Manual of Mental Disorders.* 4th ed. Washington, D.C.: American Psychiatric Association, 1994.

Asarnow, J. R., G. A. Carlson, and D. Guthrie. "Coping strategies, self-perceptions, hopelessness, and perceived family environments in depressed and suicidal children." *Journal of Consulting & Clinical Psychology* 55, no. 3 (1987): 361–66.

Bandura, A. *Self-efficacy: The Exercise of Control.* New York: W. H. Freeman, 1997.

————. *Social Foundations of Thought and Action: A Social Cognitive Theory.* Englewood Cliffs, N.J.: Prentice-Hall, 1986.

————. *Social Learning Theory.* Englewood Cliffs, N.J.: Prentice-Hall, 1977.

Bartell, N. P., and W. M. Reynolds. "Depression and self-esteem in academically gifted and nongifted children: A comparison study." *Journal of School Psychology* 24, no. 1 (1986): 55–61.

Beardslee, W. R., et al. "Examination of preventive interventions for families with depression: Evidence of change." *Development and Psychopathology* 9, no. 1 (1997): 109–30.

Beaudet, M. P. "Depression." *Health Reports* 7, no. 4 (1996): 11–25.

Beck, A. T. *Cognitive Therapy of Depression.* New York: The Guilford Press, 1979.

Beckham, E. E., and W. R. Leber, eds. *Handbook of Depression.* 2d ed. New York: The Guilford Press, 1995.

Benavidez, D., and J. L. Matson. "Assessment of depression in mentally retarded adolescents." *Research in Developmental Disabilities* 14, no. 3 (1993): 179–88.

Bernstein, D. P., et al. "Childhood antecedents of adolescent personality disorders." *American Journal of Psychiatry* 153, no. 7 (1996): 907–13.

Birmaher, B., et al. "Childhood and adolescent depression: A review of the past 10 years. Part II." *Journal of the American Academy of Child and Adolescent Psychiatry* 35, no. 12 (1996): 157–83.

Birmaher, B., R. E. Dahl, J. Perel, and B. Nelson. "Childhood and adolescent depression: A review of the past 10 years. Part I." *Journal of the American Academy of Child and Adolescent Psychiatry* 35, no. 11 (1996): 1427–35.

Boivin, M., F. Poulin, and F. Vitaro. "Depressed mood and peer rejection in childhood." *Development and Psychopathology* 6, no. 3 (1994): 483–98.

Bowlby, J. *Attachment and Loss: Vol. 1. Attachment.* 2d ed. New York: Basic Books, 1982.

————. *Attachment and Loss: Vol. 2. Separation, Anxiety and Anger.* New York: Basic Books, 1973.

————. *Attachment and Loss: Vol. 3. Loss, Sadness and Depression.* New York: Basic Books, 1980.

Brewin, C. R. "Theoretical foundations of cognitive-behavior therapy for anxiety and depression." *Annual Review of Psychology* 47 (1996): 33–57.

Brown, D. T., and H. T. Prout, eds. *Counseling and Psychotherapy with Children and Adolescents: Theory and Practice for School and Clinic Settings.* 2d ed. Brandon, Vt.: Clinical Psychology Publishing Co., 1989.

Busch, C. R., and H. P. Alpern. "Depression after mild traumatic brain injury: A review of current research." *Neuropsychology Review* 8, no. 2 (1998): 95–108.

Campbell, R. J. *Psychiatric Dictionary.* 7th ed. New York: Oxford University Press, 1996.

Cantwell, D. P., and G. A. Carlson. *Affective Disorders in Childhood and Adolescence: An Update.* New York: SP Medical & Scientific Books, 1983.

Capuzzi, D., and D. R. Gross, eds. *Youth at Risk: A Resource for Counselors, Teachers and Parents.* Alexandria, Va.: American Association for Counseling and Development, 1989.

Catania, A. C., S. R. Harnad, and B. F. Skinner. *The Selection of Behavior: The Operant Behaviorism of B. F. Skinner: Comments and Consequences.* Cambridge, N.Y.: Cambridge University Press, 1988.

Charman, T. "The stability of depressed mood in young adolescents: A school-based survey." *Journal of Affective Disorders* 30, no. 2 (1994): 109–16.

Chess, S., and A. Thomas. *Origins and Evolution of Behavior Disorders: From Infancy to Early Adult Life.* New York: Brunner/Mazel, 1984.

Chethik, M. *Techniques in Child Therapy: Psychodynamic Strategies.* New York: The Guilford Press, 1989.

Chorpita, B. F., A. M. Albano, and D. H. Barlow. "The structure of negative emotions in a clinical sample of children and adolescents." *Journal of Abnormal Psychology* 107, no. 1 (1998): 74–85.

Chorpita, B. F., and D. H. Barlow. "The development of anxiety: The role of control in the early environment." *Psychological Bulletin* 124, no. 1 (1998): 3–21.

Cicchetti, D., and S. L. Toth. "The development of depression in children and adolescents." *American Psychologist* 53, no. 2 (1998): 221–41.

———. *Developmental perspectives on depression.* Rochester, N.Y.: University of Rochester Press, 1992.

Clarizio, H. F., and K. Payette. "A Survey of School Psychologists' Perspectives and Practices with Childhood Depression." *Psychology in the Schools* 27, no. 1 (1990): 57–63.

Cohen, Lawrence H., Meredith M. Sargent, and Lee B. Sechrest. "Use of psychotherapy research by professional psychologists." *American Psychologist* 41, no. 2 (1986): 198–206.

Coles, R. *The Moral Intelligence of Children*. New York: Random House, 1997.

Compas, B. "Coping with stress during childhood and adolescence." *Psychological Bulletin* 101 (1987): 393–403.

Crowley, S. L., and E. N. Emerson. "Discriminant validity of self-reported anxiety and depression in children: Negative affectivity or independent constructs?" *Journal of Clinical Child Psychology* 25, no. 2 (1996): 139–46.

Cytryn, L., E. S. Gershon, and D. H. McKnew. "Childhood depression: Genetic or environmental influences?" *Integrative Psychiatry* 2, no. 1 (1984): 17–23.

Cytryn, L., and D. H. McKnew. *Growing Up Sad: Childhood Depression and Its Treatment*. New York: W. W. Norton, 1996.

Dalgleish, T., et al. "Information processing in clinically depressed and anxious children and adolescents." *Journal of Child Psychology and Psychiatry and Allied Disciplines* 38, no. 5 (1997): 535–41.

Dalley, M. B., et al. "Depressive symptomatology, attributional style, dysfunctional attitude, and social competency in adolescents with and without learning disabilities." *School Psychology Review* 21, no. 3 (1992): 444–58.

Dinkmeyer, D. C., and G. D. McKay. *Parenting Teenagers: Systematic Training for Effective Parenting of Teens*. 2d ed. Circle Pines, Minn.: American Guidance Service, 1990.

———. *The Parent's Handbook: STEP, Systematic Training for Effective Parenting*. 3d ed. Circle Pines, Minn.: American Guidance Service, 1989.

———. *Raising a Responsible Child: How to Prepare Your Child for Today's Complex World*. Rev. ed. New York: Simon & Schuster, 1996.

Dion, R., A. Gotowiec, and M. Beiser. "Depression and conduct disorder in native and non-native children." *Journal of the American Academy of Child and Adolescent Psychiatry* 37, no. 7 (1998): 736–42.

Eisenberg, L. "Psychiatry and health in low-income populations." *Comprehensive Psychiatry* 38, no. 2 (1997): 69–73.

Eisenberg, N. *The Caring Child*. Cambridge: Harvard University Press, 1992.

Ellason, J. W., et al. "Axis I and II comorbidity and childhood trauma history in chemical dependency." *Bulletin of the Menninger Clinic* 60, no. 1 (1996): 39–51.

Ellis, A. *Better, Deeper, and More Enduring Brief Therapy: The Rational Emotive Behavior Therapy Approach*. New York: Brunner/Mazel Publishers, 1996.

————. *How to Stubbornly Refuse to Make Yourself Miserable about Anything— Yes, Anything!* New York: Carol Publishing Group, 1990.

Ellis, A., and C. MacLaren. *Rational Emotive Behavior Therapy : A Therapist's Guide*. San Luis Obispo, Calif.: Impact Publishers, 1998.

Foster, S. *Herbs for Your Health*. Loveland, Colo.: Interweave Press, 1996.

Freud, A. *Normality and Pathology in Childhood: Assessments of Development*. New York: International Universities Press, 1965.

Friedman, R. C., and R. Corn. "Follow-up five years after attempted suicide at age 7." *American Journal of Psychotherapy* 39, no. 1 (1985): 108–13.

Fristad, M. A., B. L. Emery, and S. J. Beck. "Use and abuse of the Children's Depression Inventory." *Journal of Consulting and Clinical Psychology* 65, no. 4 (1997): 699–702.

Glynn, J., and J. A. Miller. "Suicide Prevention and Response Education (SPARE Program)." Paper presented at the Proceedings of the 1995 Annual Convention of the Texas Association of School Psychologists, Austin, Texas, 1995.

Gresham, F. M. "Best practices in social skills training." In *Best Practices in School Psychology*. A. Thomas and J. Grimes, eds. Washington, D.C.: The National Association of School Psychologists, 1992.

Hammen, C. L. *Depression Runs in Families: The Social Context of Risk and Resilience in Children of Depressed Mothers*. New York: Springer-Verlag, 1991.

Harrington, R. *Depressive Disorder in Childhood and Adolescence*. New York: Wiley, 1993.

Harrington, R., and A. Clark. "Prevention and early intervention for depression in adolescence and early adult life." *European Archives of Psychiatry and Clinical Neuroscience* 248, no. 1 (1998): 32–45.

Hart, S. L. "Childhood Depression: Implications and Options for School Counselors." *Elementary School Guidance and Counseling* 25, no. 4 (1991): 277–89.

Hershberger, W. A. "Control theory and learning theory. Special Issue: Purposeful behavior: The control theory approach." *American Behavioral Scientist* 34, no. 1 (1990): 55–66.

Herskowitz, J. "Cries for Help: Recognizing Childhood Depression." *Learning* 18, no. 5 (1990): 34–37.

Isaac, G. "Is bipolar disorder the most common diagnostic entity in hospitalized adolescents and children?" *Adolescence* 30, no. 118 (1995): 273–76.

Jensen, Joseph A., J. Regis McNamara, and Kathryn E. Gustafson. "Parents' and clinicians' attitudes toward the risks and benefits of child psychotherapy: A study of informed-consent content." *Professional Psychology: Research and Practice* 22, no. 2 (1991): 161–70.

Joiner, T. E. "The relations of thematic and nonthematic childhood depression measures to defensiveness and gender." *Journal of Abnormal Child Psychology* 24, no. 6 (1996): 803–13.

Juon, H. S., and M. E. Ensminger. "Childhood, adolescent, and young adult predictors of suicidal behaviors: A prospective study of African Americans." *Journal of Child Psychology and Psychiatry and Allied Disciplines* 38, no. 5 (1997): 553–63.

Kafantaris, V. "Treatment of bipolar disorder in children and adolescents." *Journal of the American Academy of Child and Adolescent Psychiatry* 34, no. 6 (1995): 732–41.

Kanfer, F. H., and P. Karoly. "Self-control: A behavioristic excursion into the lion's den." *Behavior Therapy* 3 (1972): 398–416.

Kaplan, C. P., and E. Shachter. "Diagnostic and treatment issues with childhood bipolar disorders." *Clinical Social Work Journal* 21, no. 3 (1993): 271–81.

Kaplan, L. J. *Adolescence: The Farewell to Childhood*. New York: Touchstone, 1984.

Kashani, J. H. "Depression in the preschool child." *Journal of Children in a Contemporary Society* 15, no. 2 (1982): 11–17.

Kaslow, N. J., and L. P. Rehm. "Childhood depression." In *The Practice of Child Therapy*. T. R. Kratochwill and R. J. Morris, eds. Needham Heights, Mass.: Allyn and Bacon, 1991.

Kaufman, J. B., et al. "Schedule for Affective Disorders and Schizophrenia for School-Age Children—Present and Lifetime Version (K–SADS–PL): Initial reliability and validity data." *Journal of the American Academy of Child and Adolescent Psychiatry* 36, no. 7 (1997): 980–88.

Kazdin, A. E. *Child Psychotherapy: Developing and Identifying Effective Treatments*. New York: Pergamon Press, 1988.

———. "Childhood depression." *Journal of Child Psychology and Psychiatry* 31, no. 1 (1990): 121–60.

Kendall, P. C., ed. *Child and Adolescent Therapy: Cognitive-Behavioral Procedures*. New York: The Guilford Press, 1991.

Kerfoot, M. "Suicide and deliberate self-harm in children and adolescents. A research update. research review." *Children & Society* 10, no. 3 (1996): 236–41.

Kovacs, M. "The Emanuel Miller Memorial Lecture 1994. Depressive disorders in childhood: An impressionistic landscape." *Journal of Child Psychology and Psychiatry and Allied Disciplines* 38, no. 3 (1997): 287–98.

Kovacs, M., and B. Devlin. "Internalizing disorders in childhood." *Journal of the American Academy of Child and Adolescent Psychiatry* 39, no. 1 (1998): 47–63.

Kovacs, M., et al. "First-episode major depressive and dysthymic disorder in childhood: Clinical and sociodemographic factors in recovery." *Journal of the American Academy of Child and Adolescent Psychiatry* 36, no. 6 (1997): 777–84.

Lonigan, C. J., M. P. Carey, and A. J. Finch. "Anxiety and depression in children and adolescents: Negative affectivity and the utility of self-reports." *Journal of Consulting and Clinical Psychology* 62, no. 5 (1994): 1000–8.

Manassis, K., and J. Hood. "Individual and familial predictors of impairment in childhood anxiety disorders." *Journal of the American Academy of Child and Adolescent Psychiatry* 37, no. 4 (1998): 428–34.

Martin, G., and J. Pear. *Behavior Modification: What It Is and How to Do It.* 5th ed. Upper Saddle River, N.J.: Prentice-Hall, 1996.

Martin, R. P. *Assessment of personality and behavior problems: Infancy Through Adolescence.* New York: The Guilford Press, 1988.

Matson, J. L. *Treating Depression in Children and Adolescents.* New York: Pergamon Press, 1989.

Maughan, B., and G. McCarthy. "Childhood adversities and psychosocial disorders." *British Medical Bulletin* 53, no. 1 (1997): 156–69.

Mazza, J. J. "School-based suicide prevention programs: Are they effective?" *School Psychology Review* 26, no. 3 (1997): 382–96.

McKnew, D. H., and L. Cytryn. "Historical background in children with affective disorders." *American Journal of Psychiatry* 130, no. 11 (1973): 1278–80.

Meichenbaum, D. *Cognitive-Behavior Modification: An Integrative Approach.* New York: Plenum Press, 1977.

———. *Exploring Choices: The Psychology of Adjustment.* Glenview, Ill.: Scott Foresman, 1988.

Meichenbaum, D., and A. Biemiller. *Nurturing Independent Learners: Helping Students Take Charge of Their Learning.* Cambridge, Mass.: Brookline Books, 1998.

Meichenbaum, D., and M. E. Jaremko. *Stress Reduction and Prevention.* New York: Plenum Press, 1983.

Meller, W. H., and C. M. Borchardt. "Comorbidity of major depression and conduct disorder." *Journal of Affective Disorders* 39, no. 2 (1996): 123–26.

Miller, A. *Prisoners of Childhood: The Drama of the Gifted Child and Search for the True Self.* New York: Basic Books, 1981.

Miller, P. A., et al. "Longitudinal study of socialization practices from preschool to early childhood." Paper presented at the Proceedings of the Annual Convention of the Society for Research in Child Development, 1991.

Morrison, H. L. *Children of Depressed Parents: Risk, Identification, and Intervention.* New York: Grune & Stratton, 1983.

Murphy, E. *The Developing Child: Using Jungian Type to Understand Children.* Palo Alto, Calif.: Consulting Psychologists Press, 1992.

Nemeroff, C. B. "The neurobiology of depression." *Scientific American* 278, no. 6 (1998): 42–49.

Nilzon, K. R., and K. Palmerus. "The influence of familial factors on anxiety and depression in childhood and early adolescence." *Adolescence* 32, no. 128 (1997): 935–43.

Nye, R. D. *Three Psychologies : Perspectives from Freud, Skinner, and Rogers.* 4th ed. Pacific Grove, Calif.: Brooks/Cole, 1992.

Pervin, L. A., ed. *Handbook of Personality: Theory and Research.* New York: The Guilford Press, 1990.

Peterson, C., S. F. Maier, and M. E. P. Seligman. *Learned Helplessness: A Theory for the Age of Personal Control.* New York: Oxford University Press, 1993.

Pine, D. S., P. Cohen, and J. Brook. "The association between major depression and headache: Results of a longitudinal epidemiologic study in youth." *Journal of Child and Adolescent Psychopharmacology* 6, no. 3 (1996): 153–64.

Pitcher, G. D., and S. Poland. *Crisis Intervention in the Schools.* New York: The Guilford Press, 1992.

Poland, S. *Suicide Intervention in the Schools.* New York: The Guilford Press, 1989.

Portegijs, P. J., et al. "A troubled youth: Relations with somatization, depression and anxiety in adulthood." *Family Practice* 13, no. 1 (1996): 1–11.

Poznanski, E. O. "Controversy and conflicts in childhood depression." *Journal of Children in a Contemporary Society* 15, no. 2 (1982): 3–10.

Proctor, R. W., and D. J. Weeks. *The Goal of B. F. Skinner and Behavior Analysis.* New York: Springer-Verlag, 1990.

Prosser, J., and P. McArdle. "The changing mental health of children and adolescents: Evidence for a deterioration?" *Psychological Medicine* 26, no. 4 (1996): 715–25.

Quinn, B. *The Depression Sourcebook.* Los Angeles: Lowell House, 1997.

Radcliffe, J., et al. "Adjustment in childhood brain tumor survival: child, mother, and teacher report." *Journal of Pediatric Psychology* 21, no. 4 (1996): 529–39.

Rehm, L. P. "A self-control model of depression." *Behavior Therapy* 8 (1977): 787–804.

Renouf, A. G., M. Kovacs, and P. Mukerji. "Relationship of depressive, conduct, and comorbid disorders and social functioning in childhood." *Journal of the American Academy of Child and Adolescent Psychiatry* 36, no. 7 (1997): 998–1004.

Reynolds, C. R., and T. B. Gutkin, eds. *The Handbook of School Psychology.* 3d ed. New York: Wiley, 1999.

Reynolds, W. M. "Depression in children and adolescents: Phenomenology, evaluation and treatment." *School Psychology Review* 13, no. 2 (1984): 171–82.

———, ed. *Internalizing Disorders in Children and Adolescents.* New York: Wiley, 1992.

Reynolds, W. M., and H. F. Johnston. *Handbook of Depression in Children and Adolescents.* New York: Plenum Press, 1994.

Rinsley, D. B. *Treatment of the Severely Disturbed Adolescent.* Northvale, N.J.: Jason Aronson, 1994.

Roberts, A. R., ed. *Crisis Intervention Handbook: Assessment, Treatment, and Research.* Belmont, Calif.: Wadsworth, 1990.

Roberts, F. M. *The Therapy Sourcebook.* Los Angeles: Lowell House, 1997.

Ronan, K. R., P. C. Kendall, and M. Rowe. "Negative affectivity in children: Development and validation of a self-statement questionnaire." *Cognitive Therapy and Research* 18, no. 6 (1994): 509–28.

Rutter, M., C. E. Izard, and P. B. Read. *Depression in Young People: Developmental and Clinical Perspectives*. New York: The Guilford Press, 1986.

Saler, L., and N. Skolnick. "Childhood parental death and depression in adulthood: Roles of surviving parent and family environment." *American Journal of Orthopsychiatry* 62, no. 4 (1992): 504–16.

Salzman, J. P. "Primary attachment in female adolescents: Association with depression, self-esteem, and maternal identification." *Psychiatry* 59, no. 1 (1996): 20–33.

Sattler, J. M. *Assessment of Children*. 3d ed. San Diego: Jerome M. Sattler, 1992.

————. *Clinical and Forensic Interviewing of Children and Families: Guidelines for the Mental Health, Education, Pediatric, and Child Maltreatment Fields*. San Diego: Jerome M. Sattler, 1998.

Scharff, D. E., and J. S. Scharff. *Object Relations Family Therapy*. Northvale, N.J.: Jason Aronson, 1991.

Seligman, M. E. P. *Helplessness: On Depression, Development, and Death*. New York: W. H. Freeman, 1992.

————. *Learned Optimism*. New York: Knopf, 1991.

Seligman, M. E. P., K. Reivich, L. Jaycox, and J. Gillham. *The Optimistic Child*. New York: HarperPerennial, 1996.

Shafii, M., and S. L. Shafii. *Clinical Guide to Depression in Children and Adolescents*. Washington, D.C.: American Psychiatric Press, 1992.

Shah, F., and S. B. Morgan. "Teachers' Ratings of Social Competence of Children with High Versus Low Levels of Depressive Symptoms." *Journal of School Psychology* 34, no. 4 (1996): 337–49.

Shirk, S. R., and R. L. Russell. *Change Processes in Child Psychotherapy: Revitalizing Treatment and Research*. New York: The Guilford Press, 1996.

Spitz, R. A., and K. M. Wolf. "Anaclitic depression; an inquiry into the genesis of psychiatric conditions in early childhood, II." *Psychoanalytic Study of the Child* 2 (1946): 313–42.

Stark, K. D. *Childhood Depression: School-Based Intervention*. New York: The Guilford Press, 1990.

Taylor, G. J., R. M. Bagby, and J. D. A. Parker. *Disorders of Affect Regulation: Alexithymia in Medical and Psychiatric Illness*. Cambridge: Cambridge University Press, 1997.

Thienemann, M., R. J. Shaw, and H. Steiner. "Defense style and family environment." *Child Psychiatry and Human Development* 28, no. 3 (1998): 189–98.

Thomas, A., and J. Grimes, eds. *Best Practices in School Psychology*. 3d ed. Washington, D.C.: The National Association of School Psychologists, 1995.

Trad, P. V. *Infant and Childhood Depression: Developmental Factors*. New York: Wiley, 1987.

Tyler, V. E. *Herbs of Choice: The Therapeutic Use of Phytomedicinals*. Binghamton, N.Y.: Haworth Press, 1994.

Webster's Medical Desk Dictionary. Springfield, Mass.: Merriam-Webster, 1986.

Weems, C. F., K. Hammond-Laurence, W. K. Silverman, and C. Ferguson. "The relation between anxiety sensitivity and depression in children and adolescents referred for anxiety." *Behaviour Research and Therapy* 35, no. 10 (1997): 961–66.

Weiss, B., K. Susser, and T. Catron. "Common and specific features of childhood psychopathology." *Journal of Abnormal Psychology* 107, no. 1 (1998): 118–27.

Whybrow, P. C. *A Mood Apart: Depression, Mania, and Other Afflictions of the Self*. New York: Basic Books, 1997.

Whybrow, P. C., and A. Parlatore. "Melancholia, a model in madness: A discussion of recent psychobiologic research into depressive illness." *International Journal of Psychiatry in Medicine* 4, no. 4 (1973): 351–78.

Winnicott, C., R. Shephard, and M. Davis, eds. *Psychoanalytic explorations: D. W. Winnicott*. Cambridge: Harvard University Press, 1989.

Wolfe, V. V., et al. "Negative affectivity in children: A multitrait-multimethod investigation." *Journal of Consulting and Clinical Psychology* 55, no. 2 (1987): 245–50.

Workman, C. G., and M. Prior. "Depression and suicide in young children." *Issues in Comprehensive Pediatric Nursing* 20, no. 2 (1997): 125–32.

Zahn-Waxler, C., and M. Radke-Yarrow. "The origins of empathetic concern." *Motivation and Emotion* 14, no. 2 (1990): 107–30.

Zeanah, C. H., ed. *Handbook of Infant Mental Health*. New York: The Guilford Press, 1993.

INDEX